YOU ARE THE
UNIVERSE

MANDALA

An Imprint of MandalaEarth
PO Box 3088
San Rafael, CA 94912
www.MandalaEarth.com

Find us on Facebook: www.facebook.com/MandalaEarth
Follow us on Twitter: @MandalaEarth

CEO Raoul Goff
Associate Publisher Phillip Jones
Editorial Director Katie Killebrew
Editorial Assistant Amanda Nelson
VP Creative Chrissy Kwasnik
Art Director Ashley Quackenbush
VP Manufacturing Alix Nicholaeff
Production Associate Tiffani Patterson
Sr Production Manager, Subsidiary Rights Lina s Palma-Temena

RAM DASS
LOVE SERVE REMEMBER
Foundation

You Are the Universe © 2022 Love Serve Remember Foundation
226 W Ojai Ave Ste. 101 #531, Ojai CA 93023

Text © 2022 Love Serve Remember Foundation
Illustrations © 2022 Amy Buetens and Julie Weinstein

Visit BeHereNowNetwork.com for insightful and entertaining podcasts.
Follow @babaramdass on Instagram, Facebook, Twitter & TikTok.

ISBN: 978-1-64722-837-8

Manufactured in China by Insight Editions
10 9 8 7 6 5 4 3 2 1

ROOTS of PEACE   REPLANTED PAPER

Insight Editions, in association with Roots of Peace, will plant two trees for each tree used in the
manufacturing of this book. Roots of Peace is an internationally renowned humanitarian organization
dedicated to eradicating land mines worldwide and converting war-torn lands into productive farms and
wildlife habitats. Roots of Peace will plant two million fruit and nut trees in Afghanistan and provide
farmers there with the skills and support necessary for sustainable land use.

RAM DASS MAPS THE JOURNEY

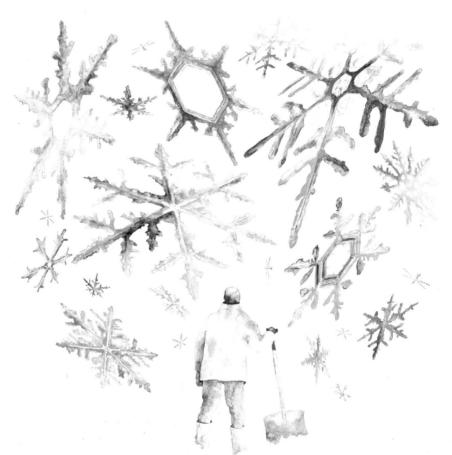

YOU ARE THE UNIVERSE

ARRANGED & ILLUSTRATED BY AMY BUETENS & JULIE WEINSTEIN

MANDALA

San Rafael • Los Angeles • London

FOR RAM DASS

For the next
generations

CONTENTS

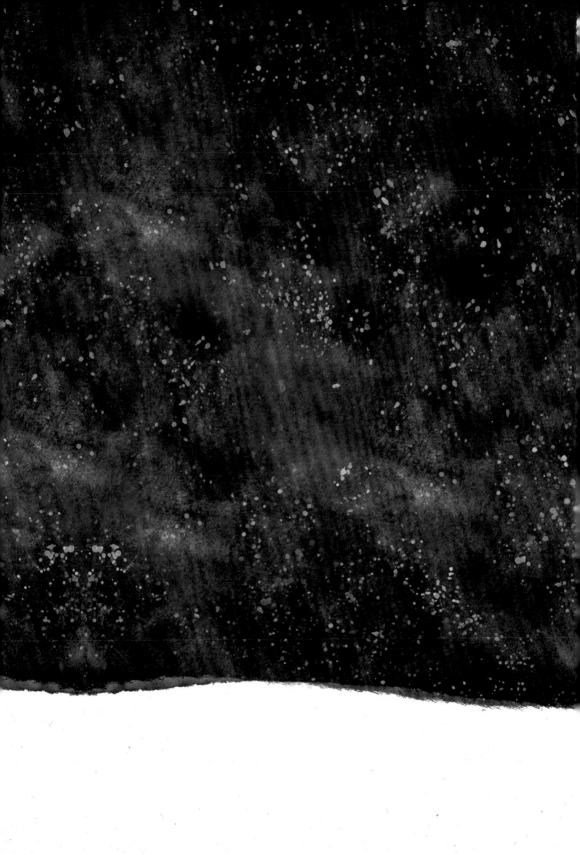

Every word you're about to read is sourced directly from Ram Dass's very own words, from fifty years of recorded lectures and interviews.

INTRODUCTION

Parallel Journeys

Friend,

I've learned that stories are such a profound way to transmit a teaching and share wisdom with other human beings. I'm not under an illusion that I have any special wisdom, but I've attempted to figure out how to live our lives out of that place of wisdom and to stay wide open to what is. I'm talking about the wisdom that has to do with the intuitive heart.

My life and my work have been about truth and teaching the truth. The nature of my work concerns the realm of human existence. What I'd like to do is present to you my own life experience and some personal reflections. I think that we can gain value out of sharing each other's stories. I always talk about myself, but it isn't really me, it's us, together. Because what awes me is how parallel our journeys are. And I just use myself as a case study that I know better than I know everybody else's case study.

I'm not selling you something or trying to convince you of anything. I'm just giving you my perception. Please understand that I'm all too human, just like you are. I get angry. I get depressed. I get everything. I screw up in human relationships. So if I say things you don't like, don't worry about them. You can take them lightly and run them through your own intuitive heart.

It's not my expectation or my hope that you would necessarily embark upon my particular journey. The spiritual journey is individual, highly personal. It can't be organized or regulated. It isn't true that everyone should follow one path. Listen to your own truth. I'm just going to tell you how I see the world, because maybe there'll be some clues in it that will be of some use to you in your own spiritual journey.

What we're really working with is to figure out how to enjoy the unfolding storyline of our life, how to delight in life, to enjoy our uniqueness, and to interact without becoming trapped in the narrowness of it. Everything changes once we identify with being the witness of the story rather than the actor in it. The witness is part of the soul, and the soul loves everything.

The soul is composed of compassion, wisdom, peace, joy, and love. This love is actually part of you. It is always flowing through you. This love is like the subatomic texture of the universe, the mysterious stuff that can't be seen, the dark matter that connects everything. You are the universe. You are never out of the flow of the universe. When you tune into that flow, you will feel it in your own heart, not your physical heart or your emotional heart, but your spiritual heart, the place you point to in your chest when you say, "I am."

We are souls having a human experience. You're a soul and I'm a soul, and this is a communication from soul to soul.

Namasté

Ram Dass

SECTION ONE

MAPPING THE JOURNEY

ONE

From Role to Soul

WHAT THE HELL?!?

My feet were on fire. I was barefoot and exhausted. I was following this guy up a winding, rocky path to a temple that I didn't want to go to in the Himalayan Mountains. Everybody is sort of ignoring me and I'm following him, running and stumbling behind a

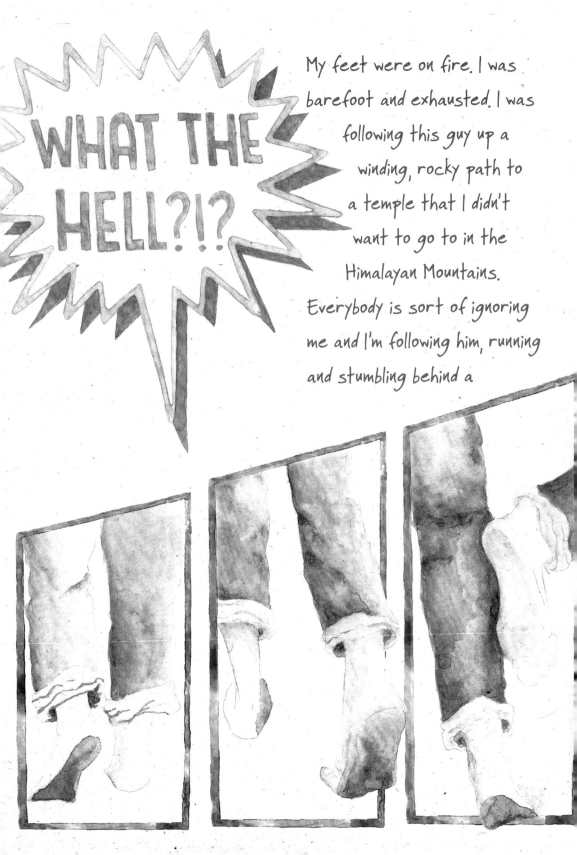

six-foot-seven giant. I'm stumbling and I'm angry and bugged, and I don't want to do this. And, we walk around a hill so that we're out of sight of the road.

HOW DID I GET HERE ?!?

We come into a hillside with a valley behind a beautiful scene and, sitting there, is a little old man with a blanket. I thought, "How did I get here?!"

I'll tell you everything. Let me start from the beginning...

Somebody Training

I was born outside of Boston, Massachusetts, on April 6, 1931, into an incredible space suit for living on this plane. This body, this was my space suit.

Like you, my space suit had a steering mechanism, with prefrontal lobes and other parts of the brain to navigate the world. And I learned my prehensile capacities, how to grab things. And I got rewarded. You get little stars and kisses and all kinds of things when you learn how to use your space suit. And you get really good at it; you get so good at using your space suit, that you can't differentiate from your space suit anymore. You think that you're your space suit. And everybody comes up and says, "What a nice suit." And you're constantly looking into other people's eyes to find out if you're really wearing a nice space suit. It's what I call somebody training. When you're born, you go into somebody training. Because your parents or guardians know who they are, and they're going to make you somebody too.

My parents were very intent on making me somebody. I was born into a wealthy Jewish family and had two older brothers. I was a cute kid named Richard Alpert. I had little blonde curls all over my head. I was an outgoing kid and loved having the attention of my relatives and friends. My parents wanted me to achieve. Be responsible. Be healthy. Be successful. Bring pride to them. And if I did what my parents wanted, I should be happy.

I wanted to be the good boy my family wanted me to be. The problem that I experienced though, was that the suit that I was wearing didn't quite fit. It was a little uncomfortable, like I needed to readjust myself. The suit didn't fit. But everybody kept saying, "Beautiful suit, really impressive suit, you must be very happy." But I wasn't. Now, if you look into everybody's eyes and they tell you you're happy and you're not, because the suit feels so weird, what do you conclude? The suit didn't fit. So I felt when everybody said, "what a nice suit" I was wearing, I thought that I must be sick.

Expectation Traps

I think that as you grow up, you become what society molds you to be. You become the child your family wants you to be, somebody who eats all their carrots. You start to develop an identity after a while, like "YOU'RE GOOD." Or "YOU'RE BAD." Or "YOU'RE A RASCAL." Or "YOU'RE..." And we carry our somebodies around with us, and it allows us to be with other people in an efficient way. The parent is under pressure to socialize the child, to make them socially functional. And in doing that, whether they intend to or not, they emotionally reward and punish the child for behaviors. This causes some feelings of unworthiness or inadequacy in most human beings who do not "fit the mold" of this type of socialization. Very few people come through socialization unharmed. I mean, that is not an unfair statement. Usually, we're left with a feeling that somehow "I'M BAD" or, "I HAVE THESE THINGS THAT ARE NOT ACCEPTABLE."

So then you build this social structure and often what you end up with is a personality that's constantly looking to others for evaluation of our behavior. And you end up asking, "DO YOU APPROVE OF ME?" "DO YOU LIKE ME?" "AM I GOOD ENOUGH?" "AM I ACCEPTABLE TO YOU?"

"HAVE I ACHIEVED ENOUGH?" "AM I A GOOD PERSON?" "AM I A BAD PERSON?" "DO I HAVE A RIGHT TO EXIST?" And we're rewarded or punished for our behavior. Then you get an A for effort, and you feel good. If you don't get the A it's not like you feel nothing, you feel bad.

DO YOU HEAR THE ISSUE THAT I'M TALKING ABOUT?

Many of us end up constantly looking into other people's eyes to find out who we are. It creates considerable anxiety because other people have their agendas, and their response to us is not always coming from a place of clarity. Their response is coming in relation to their own needs. It is not surprising then that we end up giving a considerable amount of attention to our relationships. For most people it's a very emotionally charged web we live in, and in order to feel safe and secure we attempt to place people and define them in ways that are comfortable for us. So we enter into conspiracies with one another to define each other in very simple and stable and consistent ways. Ever since I'd been born into somebody-ness, the somebody-ness had always limited who I was. I was trained to define who I was and who everybody else was. Most people learn these structures too.

You walk down the street and you're somebody. You see, you know who you are. You dress like somebody. Your face looks like somebody. Everything is somebody-ness. And the dialogue between somebodies goes, "THIS IS WHO I AM. THIS IS WHO I AM. THIS IS WHO YOU ARE. THIS IS WHO YOU ARE." Everybody is reinforcing their structure of the universe over and over again. And they meet like two huge things meeting: "THIS IS WHO I AM." "THIS IS WHO YOU ARE." We enter into these conspiracies, "I'LL MAKE BELIEVE YOU ARE WHO YOU THINK YOU ARE, IF YOU MAKE BELIEVE I AM WHO I THINK I AM." Often you can look at another person as they come down the street and see who they think they are.

We just kind of bump against each other like huge shmoos or something. You can see them in everybody. Everybody is busy being somebody.

We build our expectations about who each other is. Often we become trapped in other people's expectations about us. We learn how to treat each other in habitual ways, and we develop characteristic ways of behaving with other people. For example, a family can be a strangling type of thing that catches you or it can be a vehicle for your freedom.

This strangling feeling stayed with me throughout my teen years and into young adulthood. It was horrible, but when I look back I see how it deepened my being. You will see that there are many different levels of spiritual evolution, which has to do with the human spirit or soul. They are merely stages of development, similar to physical and mental stages of development. Be careful not to impose values of better or worse. I learned it's no better to be an adolescent than to be a child. It is no better to be an old person than middle aged. These are just different stages of development, but I didn't see it that way back then.

I had a lot of unhappiness that started around puberty. In junior high, I was funneled into a school with kids from different ethnic and religious backgrounds, including many Jews, like myself. Now I know that there are things about Judaism in terms of a quality of emotion and love of intellect, a quality of compassion and an understanding of suffering, that are deep within me, but as a kid, being

Jewish was another area of my life that I wrestled with. I wasn't born into Judaism by accident, but as a kid I didn't know how to honor that, nor did I have the courage, the chutzpah, to question it. Anyway, I was a fat Jewish kid, and the other kids would beat me up. I would have milkshakes with my teachers, and the bus driver let me be the doorman, so I had peers, but not friends. Then I was off at a prep school for rich, conservative kids and I was so miserably unhappy and neurotic. It was the unhappiest period of my life.

I wanted friends to accept and like me, but sometimes I felt lonely. I thought that having friends and lovers was the solution to loneliness. I thought, "Oh, if it was only different from this." And the little flip had not yet occurred to me to look at things just the way they are, without expectations and without preconceived models. I tried to get rid of these feelings by surrounding myself with other people. Later I realized that wasn't the solution. I wish I knew back then that it's alright to be lonely. I got to a point where I wasn't lonely much of the time anymore, but when I was, I just allowed it to be. I just sat and felt lonely knowing the feeling would eventually pass.

15

When I was in prep school, I was caught wrestling naked with one of my male classmates. We were spied on by seniors. Everyone found out, and I was completely ostracized by the whole school. Nobody would talk to me. I was humiliated. Finally, the captain of the swim team decided to be my friend. That was a very kind thing of him.

Sexual confusion, especially in the teenage years, is more natural than I knew. I take comfort in younger generations that celebrate the rainbow of sexual expression. I applaud the removal of that stigma I struggled with so much.

After that, I never wanted to make my sexuality known, even into an adulthood, because I didn't want people to be distracted from my message, to fixate on my sexuality, and miss the truth I wanted to share. My homosexuality was the one thing I had not been truthful about, until I knew how important it is to be honest. I remember a quote by Mahatma Gandhi: "Only God is truth. I am a human being. Truth for me is changing every day. My commitment must be to truth, not to consistency."

Back then and for many years I was not truthful or consistent. I had a girlfriend, and I did the whole double life thing. I always felt like I was acting, whether I was with straight or gay people. I mean I did it, but the feeling was just crap. It's not what I would have chosen to do, but it always pulled

me into the witness or into that part of
my mind which is a neutral observer, just
noticing and not judging or criticizing.

I mean, eventually I came to see my sexuality as being an asset. I didn't ask for it,
and I wouldn't ask for it again. I want you to know,
I'm not gonna kid myself, but it's the way it went down.
It took me many years to just say, "I am what I am. And it's tough shit if you
don't like it, that's your problem." I am what I am, and sometimes I'm turned on
by a man and sometimes I'm turned on by a woman. And, if I'm gonna go to hell, I'm
gonna go to hell. But that's the way it is.

I started to appreciate my humanity. When I allowed myself to be what I am,
without that negative dislike of myself, things changed much faster. I mean,
things fell away more quickly. I could feel change occurring in myself and then
I would start to experience my own beauty, and it frightened me because it
didn't correspond with the model that I had cultivated of myself over the
years, that I had to do good in order to be beautiful.

I want to tell you something: You are loved just for being
who you are, just for existing. You don't have to do anything
to earn it. Your shortcomings, your lack of self-esteem,
physical perfection, or social and economic success. None
of that matters. No one can take this love away from you,
and it will always be here.

To the extent that somebody has had a lot of shit go down about their being gay, or any kind of conflict, for that matter, and has gone through a lot of suffering and so on, it can seem like a total drag when it's happening and feel overwhelming, but I look back now and I see that this planted the seed for what would become my compassion. That's not to say I would have asked for that experience. I hated it while it was happening. I was full of self-pity and doubt, fury, and anger, and I couldn't tell my parents.

Like I said, it was horrible, but it deepened my being. It threw me back in on myself while a lot of people who stayed outside of themselves, who appeared to be loved by everybody and were having success, stayed very external. I've had a very deep inward life, not just because of that, but because of all the things that happened to me, all the beings in my life, and the experiences along the way.

I hadn't yet made the connection that these painful experiences had a cer-tain function. I didn't know how to use these experiences intentionally and consciously as a vehicle through which I could awaken to who I am, in truth. But during this period of my life, I started to open to who I really was, and to who you really are.

Outgrowing the Costume

When I was maybe nine or so, in my family, the best thing to want to be was a doctor. To them, that was really somebody.

And everybody rewarded you with microscopes, and books, and patted you on the head, and smiled. And I milked that one until I was well into college and was flunking biology and

chemistry, until the moment of truth came when I announced that I would not do what my family expected of me. I wanted to take a different route.

For the first thirty or thirty-five years of my life I was busy putting myself down, but I had begun to open to the process of awakening that says, "START FROM WHERE YOU ARE. ALLOW YOURSELF TO BE WHERE YOU ARE. STOP JUDGING YOURSELF SO MUCH, PUTTING YOURSELF DOWN SO HARD. STOP TRYING TO FORCE YOURSELF INTO MODELS OF HOW YOU THINK YOU OUGHT TO BE. JUST BE WHAT YOU ARE." And I started to just be honest about my life.

I have led three lives. I have three chapters, each of which has led quite naturally into the next. Although at times it didn't seem very natural. The first chapter was that of being a social scientist, therapist, and wealthy professor at four major universities. The second was that of being an ex-plorer in the psychedelic community. And the third is that of being a student of yoga on a spiritual path.

I was at the height of my career and climbing the academic ladder pretty fast. I had a busy social life and was amassing a lot of money. I had collected all of the symbols of success in society. Or at least a large number of them. My apartment was full of antiques. I had my pilot's license and a Cessna airplane, a Triumph motorcycle, a Mercedes-Benz, an MG sports car, silk jackets, a sailboat, the works. I felt myself being a model of what should be in our culture. People were always complimenting me saying, "You're so successful. You've turned out to be somebody special! You're a good role model."

So I thought I was becoming well known and powerful in my roles, and that all of my hard work and training to become somebody was really paying off. Although it looked awfully good on paper, there was something wrong inside about it. Every now and then, just before I'd be going to sleep or when I'd be in the bathtub or something, there'd be a moment when there wasn't somebody else's eyes to look into to tell me how wonderful I was. And I knew that it wasn't enough.

Standing Outside of Myself

I had a big corner office at Harvard with two secretaries and about forty research assistants. Down the hall, in a little closet-like place, there was this other guy, the new research psychologist. We became friends and co-workers and he invited me to fly to Mexico to meet him and a few others for summer vacation. A few days before I arrived, my new friend had just had this experience in which he had taken the sacred mushrooms of Mexico, called teonanacatl mushrooms, meaning flesh of the gods, which were given to him by an Indigenous folk healer.

I heard many stories about what happened to him. He said he had learned more in this one experience than he had in all of his years as a psychologist.

All over the world, for thousands of years, certain plants have been used as medicines and in cultural ceremonies. We had just learned about them. I was interested to try some for myself but there weren't any more of the mushrooms around. We flew back to the United States together in my plane, with his son and new pet iguana, and he went back to Harvard to start exploring these chemicals, which at the time were not illegal. We wanted to continue studying the many dimensions of personality, social relationships and human consciousness. So I was quite eager to have this experience and he had gotten hold of the synthetic version of psilocybin mushrooms.

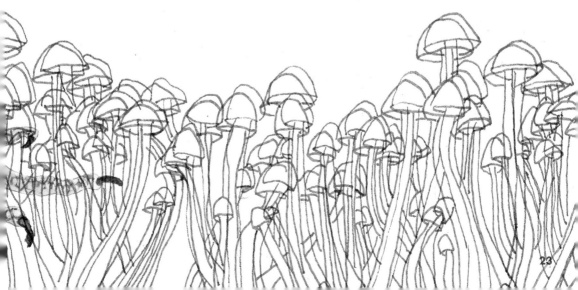

On March 6, 1961, the night of Cambridge, Massachusetts's biggest snowstorm of the year, I discovered that there's much more in any given moment than we usually perceive. That we ourselves are much more than we usually perceive. When you know that, part of you can stand outside the drama of our life.

FROM THIS,
I'VE LEARNED THAT

I AM
NOT THIS BODY.
I AM *IN* THIS BODY.

THIS IS PART OF
MY INCARNATION AND
I HONOR IT
BUT THAT ISN'T
WHO I AM.

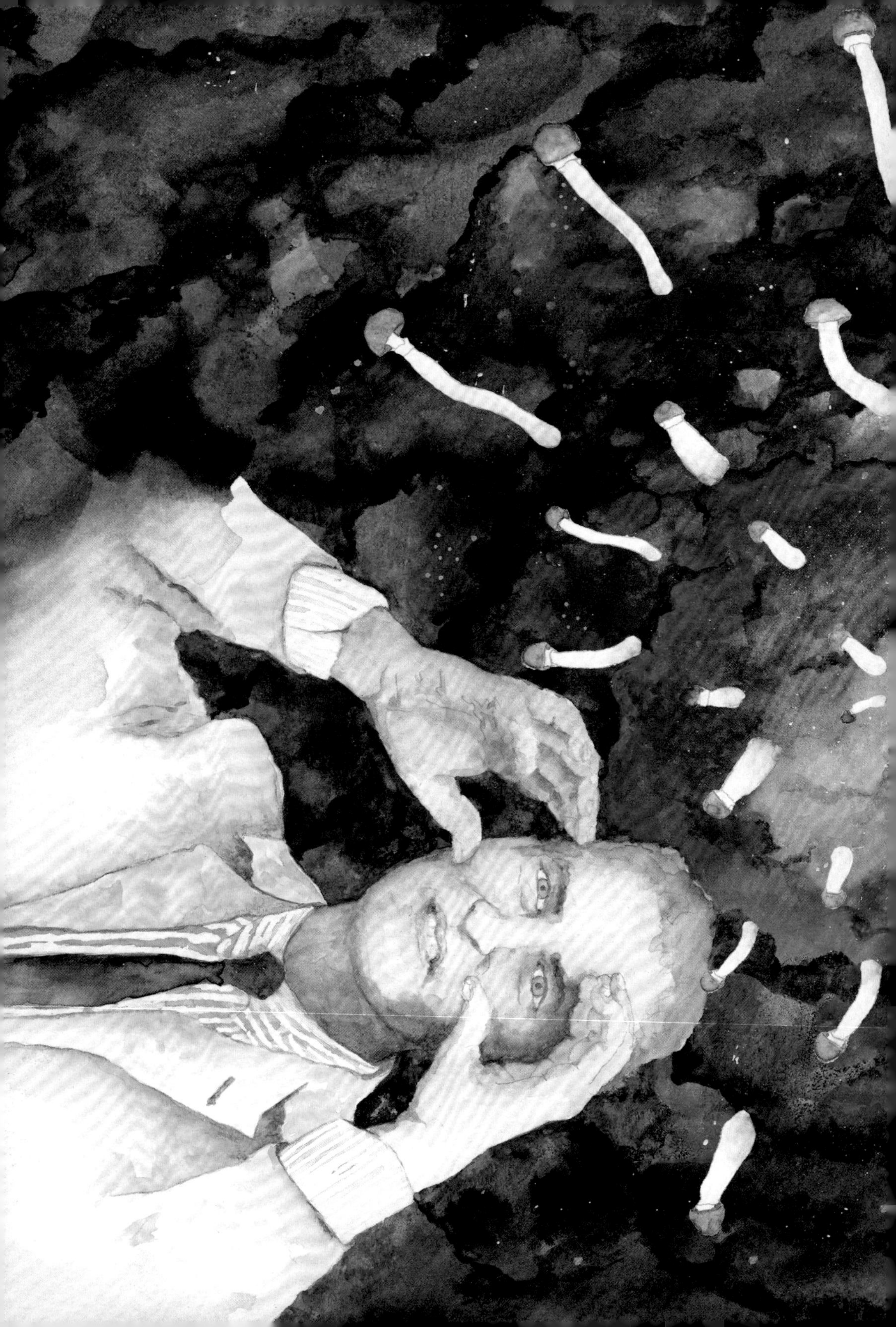

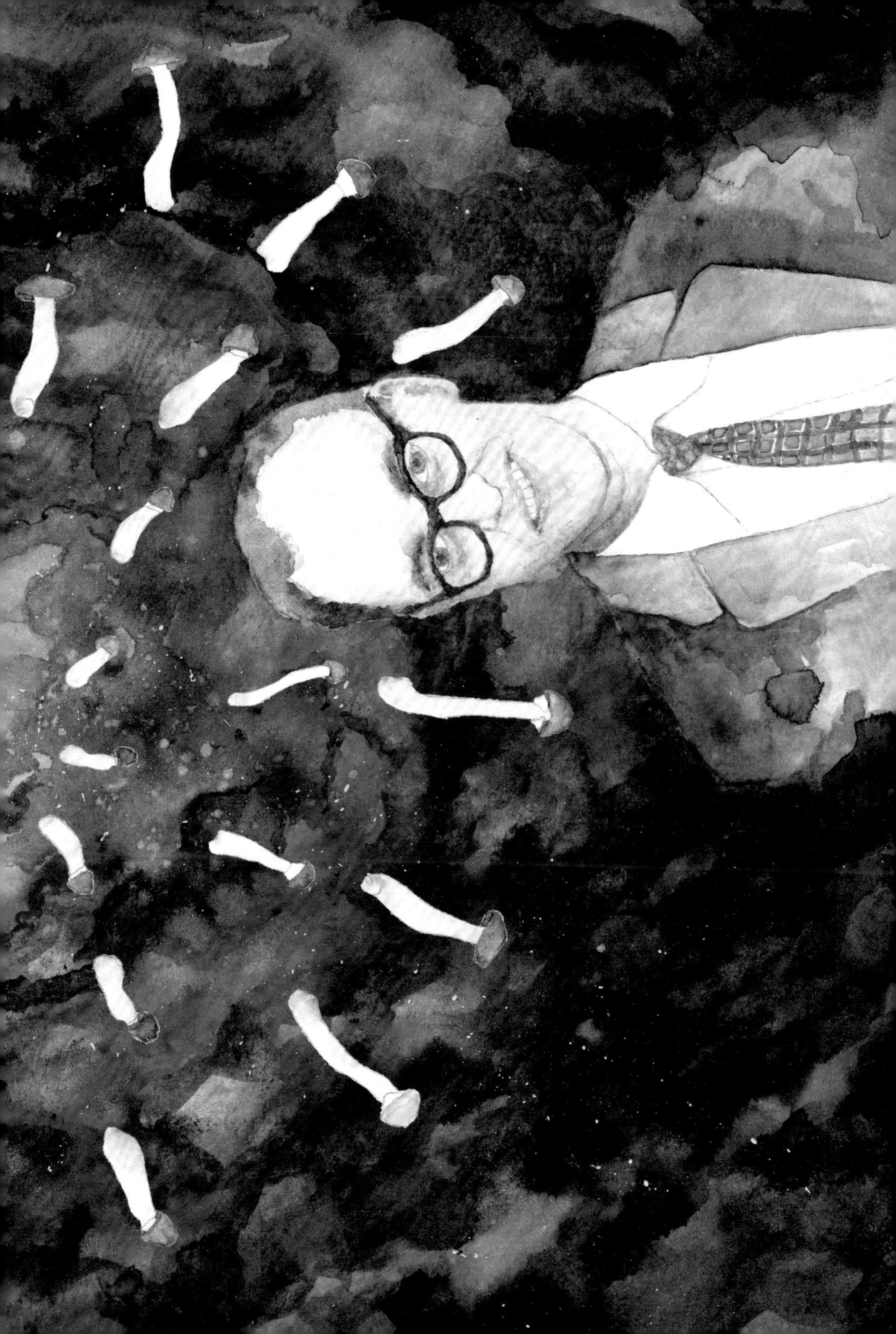

That night I went to my parents' house to visit them, and then I trudged two blocks through the snow over to my friend's house to try this new chemical. Initially the first part of the experience had a certain unpredictability about it, and I felt uncomfortable. But a few hours later I went off into the living room, and I sat in the semidarkness by myself to reflect upon these new feelings and senses. A deep calm pervaded my being. The rug appeared to be moving and the pictures were smiling. The light came in from the street. It was snowing and it was very beautiful. I was sitting there and suddenly in the dark across the room I saw a figure standing there, where a moment before there had been no one. I thought, "How interesting...an external hallucination." As I looked more closely, I realized that the figure was none other than myself. I, it, was dressed in a cap and gown, strangely enough, and what I saw was my 'professor-ness' across the room. It was as if that part of me that was a Harvard professor had separated or disassociated itself from me. And so I looked at this professor-ness and I said, "Well." And I wasn't me any longer. I mean, I was here and there was it, and I said, "Well, I worked hard for that status, but I guess I don't really need that anymore. So I'll give it up." And I sat back and relaxed.

The minute I said, "I don't need that anymore," the figure changed, and it was somebody else. I sat forward and there I was again, except now I was the young, popular socialite. My socialiteness was sitting over there. I thought, "All right. I guess I can do without that." And in a sequential order, I went by all of my social roles: lover, wise man, kind person, all my roles. And to each one I said, "OK." "Too bad about that one." "OK, there 'it' goes."

Then came the role of Richard Alpert. That is, the basic social identity by which I had always acknowledged my existence. Well now, this was a different matter! You see, this was who I learned to be way back then, and I wasn't at all sure what would happen if I gave that up. I thought, "What kind of drug have I taken?! What has this madman given me?!" See, I'd already made it someone else's fault, not mine.

I was certain I would have amnesia, because I thought I was losing my identity and I won't know who I am. I said, "Alright. Well. I can always get another social identity." I went through this thought process. "I'll give up Richard Alpert-ness, but at least I have my body." But I had spoken too soon. I looked down at the couch. Nothing below my knees was visible any longer. As I watched, slowly it all disappeared until there was only the couch on which I was sitting.

I experienced a kind of panic in that moment. There was nothing in my model of the universe that led me to believe that if I was not in my body there would be anything left. So as far as I was concerned, I was dying or ceasing to exist. That was it.

And I recall the feeling. I recall the adrenaline flowing. I recall the sweat breaking out. I recall wanting to scream out for help. I recall all those feelings. As the panic was mounting, in whatever it is that it was mounting in, since I wasn't seeing anything, a voice inside of me said very quietly and rather playfully, "But who's minding the store?" And I became aware at that moment that everything by which I knew myself to be was gone, including life as I knew it. Still, I was fully aware. Still there was something in me that was watching this whole process disappear. There was what I was calling at the time, a scanning device or a point of awareness. Something in there that had no reference to body, no reference to personality, no reference to any of my social roles, and yet there it was clear and lucid and watching the whole thing. A witness. You know? Just watching it all happen.

Instantly, with this recognition I felt a new kind of calmness, one of a profundity never experienced before. I had just found that I. That which was I was beyond life and death. It was wise rather than just knowledgeable. It was a voice inside that spoke truth. And the minute I defined it or labeled it, or named it, I experienced a tremendous exhilaration and feeling of liberation. I became pure spirit, pure consciousness and love. I experienced a feeling that everything was interconnected in the universe. Fear turned to exaltation. Metaphorically I took off my suits entirely, I let go of all of my roles, and it felt wonderful. Absolutely wonderful. I felt at home. I felt at peace. I felt content.

I ran out in the snow and danced before I found my way back through the snowdrifts to my parents' home around five in the morning. I decided to shovel the snow. My parents opened the window and shouted, "You damned idiot, come in! You don't shovel snow in the middle of the night." I looked up and I heard this voice coming from within, and I listened to the voice inside say, "It's cool if you want to shovel snow. It's alright. Nothing immoral about that. It's alright." I looked up at them and I smiled, and I danced a bit of a jig and I went back to shoveling. The window closed and I saw them smiling behind it.

Well now, I was presented with a peculiar dilemma. Because, the next Monday when I had to get up and give my class lectures in human motivation and theory of ego psychology, I saw my words were not adequate to the experience that I had. Because that place that I had gone to, I couldn't find it anywhere in books. And I couldn't find the words to tell anybody about what had happened. This was an ineffable experience. I thought, "I'd like to tell ya about it, but it's ineffable, sorry."

I began to share what I learned with my students, but Harvard didn't agree with my lessons. Ultimately we were fired and free to continue to research and teach as we pleased.

Until 1961 I was quite certain I was who my parents had told me who I was. I was somebody. I was Richard. I was good, I was an achiever. In other words, I was identified with my personality. I was also a professor. I was a cellist. I was a pilot. And I enjoyed all of those identities as well. I think it's most likely that I would have gone along at that pace just collecting more and more baggage, but this experience gave me a new consciousness, a new perspective from my heart. Before, I was just a set of roles. Nothing behind it. They didn't add up to the feeling of home, of being comfortable in myself. I was outgrowing the need to constantly look at other peoples' eyes to see whether I was doing good, and I felt freed from other people's judgments on my actions. This experience freed me. It changed my life, it completely altered my point of view. I saw the universe from a different vantage point. I saw a part of myself that made me question the whole social structure and not be willing to play by the rules anymore. In other words, I met something behind my own ego. I became identified with the spiritual being inside of myself. I spent the rest of my life growing into what I learned from that first experience.

The psychedelic experience isn't necessarily for everybody, and we need to be sensitive to this. I want to be clear, psychedelics are subject to incredible misuse, especially when they're not approached sacramentally or consciously. It's better if you wait to become SOMEBODY before you try to become NOBODY. Most kids use drugs before their egos are settled. Because they use them prematurely, they lose their ground, and could even lose their ability to function in society. I honored psychedelics as a method, but I say there are other methods. The game isn't to get high, the game is to become free.

Searching for the Map

In 1961 I found out I wasn't who I thought I was, but that I was actually much more interesting than who I thought I was. Despite this realization, several psychedelic sessions, and a lot of therapy, there was a gnawing uneasiness that I was still missing something. I continued feeling very dissatisfied and unhappy.

It was becoming clear to me that for all our idealistic aspirations we didn't know enough about using these plant substances and chemicals. The highs and lows of psychedelic sessions had not led to stable results in our lives. Although we had experienced profound insights and ecstatic states, we were not able to translate them into enduring enlightenment. We did not really know how to integrate these illuminations into life. We needed a map for this journey, and practices. I was not getting any new information from the sessions, and when I was alone I went into a very deep depression.

I saw that my discomfort was a deeper something in me attempting to awaken. And that maybe instead of treating my discomfort as some sickness that ought to be treated as a problem, I should see it as something graceful to be honored. And maybe it would be useful to allow my life to adapt, to tune to those feelings of wrongness or rightness within myself.

At some point I assume that you, too, will experience this, if you haven't already. Awakening is the realization that the whole constellation of thoughts of who you think you are is a very limiting condition, and that you are much, much more than that. That the model of who you thought you were was just that: a model. It was a model of reality, and it was just a model. It wasn't **THE** model. Just A model. It's a perspective shift in which you see that reality is not absolute, it's relative. **IS THIS TOO WEIRD FOR EVERYONE?** Many of us have experienced states of transcendence, an altered state of consciousness. And once we've experienced them, our lives are different. Once you've recognized that there are other realities than the one you've been familiar with, your life starts to change. I don't care whether you got it from a joint, whether you got it from meditation, making art, or volunteering, whether you got it from sex, whether you got it from trauma, whether you got it from surfing, or whatever. Whatever thing you did that took you beyond yourself, like you could have gotten it from religious ecstasy in temple or church, you could have gotten it in a thousand different ways; whatever it was, if you acknowledged it as real, you are on the way. From then on, you literally cannot fall off the path of awakening. You can think you fell off the path, which many people do, but you can't.

During this period of my life, I became aware of the East, which includes parts of Asia. It's a different culture. I learned more about the wisdom they held from friends and books passed along to me. I was a Westerner interested in Eastern spirituality and religions and began to study Buddhism and Hinduism. Eastern philosophy teaches us to go inward, deepening our understanding of ourselves.

Many people, including me and possibly you, appreciate that there could be multiple realities existing at the same time, beyond our normal waking state of consciousness. There is a very ancient tradition of people from Eastern cultures who have realized other states of consciousness and have sent messages and made maps that describe different levels of awareness. I was grateful to learn that they understood different planes of awareness, something that Western psychology didn't really address. This made me think the East was better connected with the planes of consciousness. I'd been longing to understand these different planes of consciousness I'd experienced since that night of the snowstorm. I was looking for somebody that could read the maps of my soul's consciousness. So I decided to go to India.

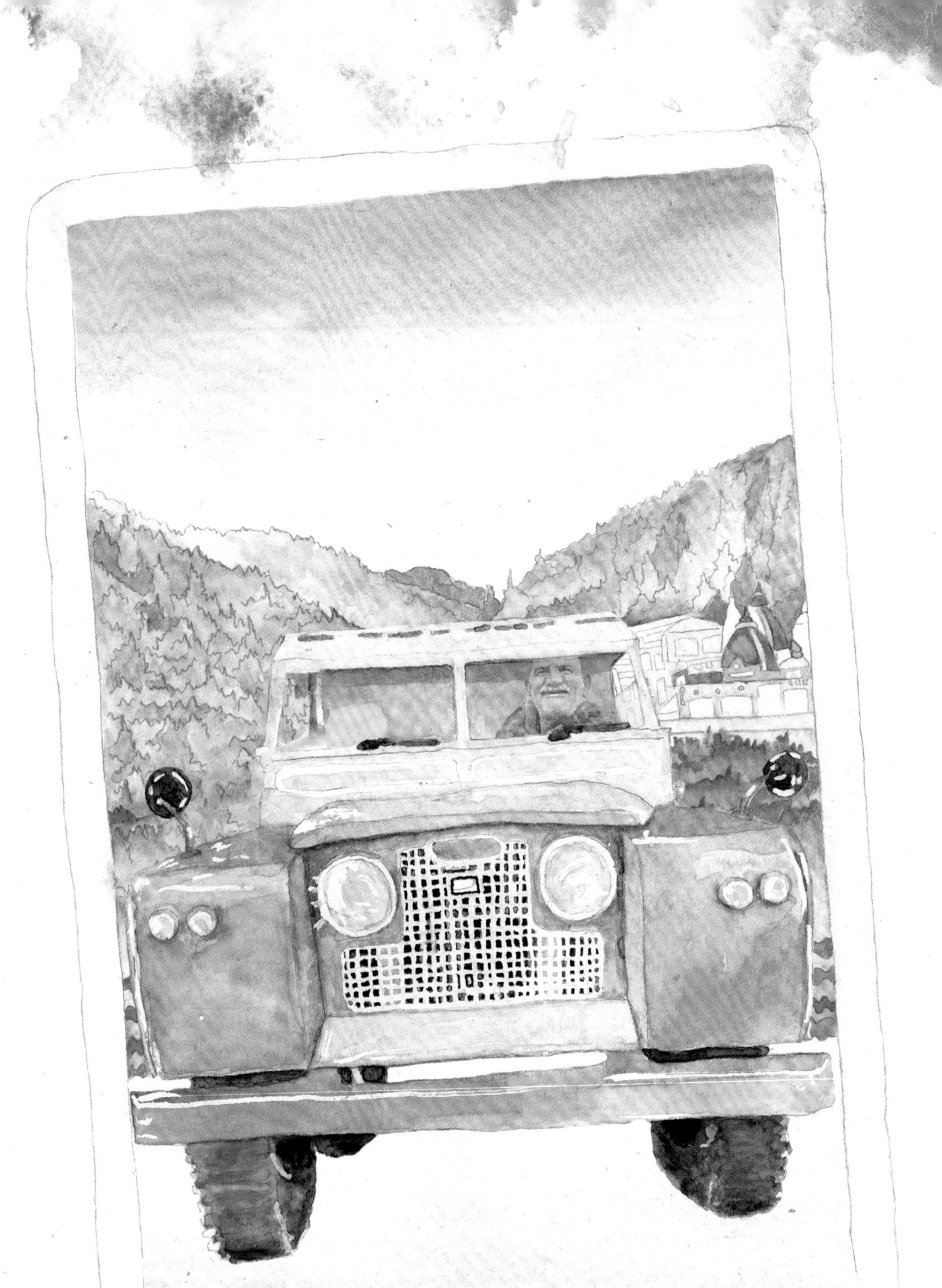

The Guide and Compass:
Home Sweet Home

I got to India. We had traveled overland for several days and we stopped near a lake to camp. I woke up in the middle of the night and I couldn't fall back to sleep. I went outside to pee and was looking up at the sky. The stars were very bright. I was thinking about my mother who had just died six months earlier.

I felt very close to her at that moment, like when you get out in the universe and you feel close to things that you are spiritually linked to. That was the first time I had ever thought about my mother in a spiritual way. I went back to bed and I didn't tell anybody about this.

The next morning after camping at the lake, we began our trek up the mountain to a little temple in the Himalayas.

ALRIGHT, now we're all caught up in the story. As I was saying in the beginning...

So I'm begrudgingly stumbling up this trail, way up in the mountains. There's no electricity up here, it's very remote. I'm trying to keep up with the guy I'm with, and I'm being ignored by everybody, and I'm just in terrible shape, really stumbling up this path. I'm angry and bugged, and I don't want to do this, and we walk around a hill so that we're out of sight of the road.

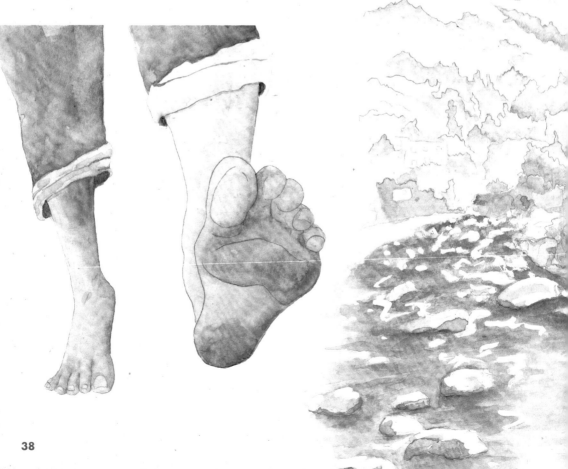

It's a sunny day, and we come into a hillside with a valley behind a picturesque scene. There was a beautiful tree, and sitting under the tree was an old man with a blanket wrapped around him, and about thirty people sitting with him. People call him Maharajji, a common term used in India for a great saint. His name is Neem Karoli Baba.

I stopped and waited and just looked on. I was paranoid about the whole scene, didn't want to meet this old man and didn't understand why everyone was touching his feet. I didn't believe in gurus and all that crap. He pointed at me and he spoke. I couldn't understand him. I kept my hands in my pockets when he called me over to sit down with him.

The next thing that happened blew my mind. After a little while he looked at me with a twinkle and said, "You were out thinking about your mother last night?" And I thought, "Whoa. That's very unusual." I've studied cognitive psychology and we can't do any of that. And I said, "Yes that's right." "She got big in the stomach?" "Yes," I said. He said, "Your mother died a few months ago." And he was saying all this in Hindi. "She died of spleen." Spleen was one word he spoke in English, so the word spleen hit me. How did he know this?! I had become very close with my mother in the past few years. So when he said to me, "She is a saint," I was mystified that he knew her in this way. Nothing made me ready for that.

He had shown me that he read my mind. I had never experienced anything like that. I thought, "My God, he's going to know all the things I don't want people to know." I was really embarrassed, because I thought if people knew me, they wouldn't like me. When I first met my guru, I thought, "If he only knew." Then I realized that he did know, even my darkest and most shameful faults. He knew, and he loved me.

I looked up and he was looking at me with unconditional love. I had never been looked at that way. Not by my parents, friends, lovers. Not by anybody. I felt love, and I felt something happening in my heart. He was a few inches from my face, just staring directly at me. At that moment I felt this incredibly violent wrenching in my chest as if a screeching door was being opened. It was like a very severe pain in my heart. I felt a painful feeling inside of me and began to cry uncontrollably.

I wasn't crying because I was sad, and I wasn't crying because I was happy. I was just crying. And it was very bewildering, but not uncommon, because it takes us a long time, many of us longer than others, to come up out of the darkness of our feelings of unworthiness, of unlovableness, of feeling safe to be in the presence of love. The closest way I could describe it was that I was crying because I was home. Home in my heart. It was all okay. He transferred my identity to my real self, just by looking at me with love. I cried for two days, and they took good care of me and they fed me. The Indians are beautiful, wonderful people.

In my first meeting with him, Maharajji showed me his powers. He blew my mind that he knew about my mother and that I was thinking about her the night before. At that point, I was impressed with his mind reading. He blew my mind first, so he could get the mind out of the way. But I realized that it was really his unconditional love that pulled me in. This helped me see that I could accept myself as lovable, and my fear started to dissolve. I started to allow the truth of who I was. After that, all I wanted to do was share that love.

Unconditional love really exists in each of us. It's part of our deep inner being. It is not so much an active emotion as a state of being. It's not "I love you" for this or that reason, not "I love you if you love me."

Going to India, after the psychedelics, I came into a culture that recognized spirit. In India they have an expression, "GOD, GURU AND SELF ARE ONE IN THE SAME." The way we use the term GURU in the West, since we don't understand it very well, is like a sort of super teacher. We make it into sort of a glorified teacher, and that isn't really what a guru is, not from my point of view. A guru is like a door frame through which you see truth. There are a lot of people who present themselves as gurus, and that has nothing to do with whether they're gurus or not, in the real sense of the term guru. The difference is that A TEACHER POINTS THE WAY; THE GURU IS THE WAY. I see him as a doorway toward God. All he wanted was for people to be liberated, to be free.

After I met my spiritual teacher, my whole life took a different turn again. I mean, mushrooms did it the first time, he did it the second time. That experience changed me. That first visit lasted six months. I ended up living in a temple, studying Hindu philosophy, doing deep meditation, hatha yoga, and so on, and I began to understand a different context for what life and death was about. I was beginning to find answers to the questions I had come to India with.

I went to India because I was looking for somebody who could read the maps of my consciousness. I found Maharajji. He was the map. I remember that first visit with my guru. It felt like I was home. The search was over. This moment would serve as the guide and compass for my life's journey forward.

Truth. Love. Consciousness. That's what God is to me. It's just consciousness.

TWO

From
Head to
Heart

Love Everyone
and Tell the Truth

Maharajji said I should stay in the West and not talk to anybody about him. Well, during those first two years I talked about nothing but him. When I came back from India, I gave lectures to large audiences throughout the country. I tried to capture in words the examples he gave us to live a life of purpose, including to "love everyone, and tell the truth."

In those early days of being with Maharajji, he would tell me repeatedly, "Ram Dass, I want you to love everybody and tell the truth." It was like he was telling me that the person I thought myself to be was changing. He was changing my insides. He came up to me, nose to nose, looked me in the eye, and said, "Give up anger. You tell the truth and you love everybody." At that time, I could only do that every now and then. We treat love and hate and the other emotions like they are all on the same level, but they're not. Hate, fear, lust, greed, jealousy — all that comes from the ego. I was living most of the time on the ego plane of consciousness. I could love almost everyone for short periods of time, but the truth was that I did not love everyone. I told him I couldn't do that, because of my ego and judgments. But he didn't care.

He was telling me to take a different path and identify with my soul, because the soul loves everybody and tells the truth. The soul is another level of who we are, a different plane of consciousness. What he was saying is that when I can relate from the soul's plane of consciousness, which is who I really am, then I will love everyone. That is my truth. That's the best thing I can do to affect the entire universe. Only love comes from the soul. I was learning that when you identify with your soul, you live in a loving universe. You can feel it in your heart. It's like the sun.

It brings out the beauty in each of us. It took me nearly half of my life to identify with my soul, but I don't think it takes everybody fifty years.

I was lucky to have a spiritual community that I could explore what it meant to see others as souls and to travel the spiritual path with. This became my **satsang**, my community of like-minded souls who were also interested in living a life in search of universal truths. Satsang became my chosen family that I could share spiritual practices with, make bread and break bread with, chant mantra and sing **kirtan** with and get to know what it really meant to love everyone, as a soul, unconditionally. I used to say, "If you think you're enlightened, go spend a week with your family." I didn't identify with my biological family as my spiritual community, but satsang can very similarly bring up family triggers. Our satsang became very close friends, and I loved them all, but there was a time when I'd look at them sometimes and think, "What am I doing with this crowd?!" But the thing was, Maharajji could look at them and just see them as souls, he wasn't looking at their incarnation. Even though I absolutely treasured satsang, I had plenty of opportunities to practice giving up anger and judgment, and loving everyone as a soul.

It was challenging for me to figure out what "love everyone" really meant. Don't get me wrong, as a soul you can love everyone, but you can and should work to become conscious enough to know when to withdraw yourself from the chain of reactivity and remove yourself from drama. It was clear that I had to let go of stuff to be able to do that. Sometimes it took me three breaths instead of two, but I got to the point where I could do it. People go around carrying everybody's stuff all of the time; I definitely did. Once I stopped clinging, I was able to just pick it up and put it back down. That doesn't mean I'm not compassionate, it doesn't mean I don't love people. We can still love everyone but holding onto people's suffering is not compassionate for them or for you. To not be trapped in the stuff of life, it takes some effort, discipline and work with one's mind. The earlier you start, the less you're going to be trapped later on in the daily stuff of what we call suffering.

Learning to love everyone brought another challenge. I'm sure you can relate. You may ask, "How do I love someone if I don't like them?" Well, I figured out that if I can see the soul that happens to have incarnated into a person that I don't care for, then I remind myself to love their soul and not their role. I think that's what his instructions to love everyone really mean. For example, it's liberating to resist another person politically, yet still see them as another soul. Like particular politicians are full of shoddy, manipulative deceit. I also know they are fellow souls, just like I am, and that they can grow, just like we can all grow, so I worked to keep my mind and heart soft and open and receptive to allow them to grow, because it's for our own survival. When somebody is doing actions you don't like, the spiritual solution is to say, "I don't agree with that action you're about to do, and in fact I'm going to try to peacefully stop you from doing the action," but you do it in such a way that you do not reject the person. YOU REJECT THE ACTION, BUT NOT THE PERSON. That's a big one; it's worth saying again. You reject the action, but not the person. Maharajji said to me, "You don't have to change anybody, you just have to love them." Love the soul, not the role. Because he knew that love is the most powerful medicine.

"Love everyone" is hard, but "tell the truth" is also tough. There are just so many little lies in our daily life to make other people more comfortable, because we don't want to hurt the other person, because we want to trade off kindness for truth, and that kindness leaves you isolated. I hate to say that, I mean it's bizarre to say that, because isn't it important to be kind? Most relationships are a conspiracy saying, "I won't upset your ego, if you don't upset mine." And most families survive by doing that. But I think that if you speak the truth, consistently, and if it's done with love and mutual respect, you can end up just in a liquid space of appreciation together. However, I also

"Love everyone" is hard, but "tell the truth" is also tough.

Truth

realized that living in truth does not mean telling everybody everything that you think, because most people don't want to know the truth. But it does mean being truthful with yourself, and with other people, if they are willing.

Truth is the basic fabric of the universe. The truth is everywhere. Wherever you are, it's right where you are.

Tell the truth. Wow, it's hard. Total honesty with ourselves, total honesty is the key. Whenever I've chosen something that is not true to my being, I've ended up angry and frustrated because I picked wrong. If we make a mistake, admit it and get on with it. Don't cover errors. The whole spiritual journey is a continuous act of falling on our faces. And we get up, brush ourselves off and get on with it. We can't be afraid of making errors.

After a lifetime of not telling the truth, I learned to use my role as a public speaker to make my truth as available as I possibly could for those that wanted to hear it.

Be Here Now

Out of these lectures came BE HERE NOW, the first book I wrote after I returned from India. Many people told me how BE HERE NOW had changed their life. See, BE HERE NOW wasn't my book. One day, when I was with my guru, a yogi was present and he said, "Maharajji gave his asherbad for your book." Asherbad means blessing. I wasn't writing a book. But I thought I'd better start writing one soon. And his blessing was that book. And that book changed probably millions of hearts. I was just a bystander. People would say, "I enjoyed your book." And I'd say, "It's his book."

50

Really, the book came together with the help from satsang who were living at my friends' commune in Taos, New Mexico called the Lama Foundation. The Lama Foundation is a beautiful mountain retreat center where people of all faiths come to explore spiritual practices and religious traditions in community and connect to the land. It was one of the first retreat centers I ever taught at. BE HERE NOW came together in the most incredible way. A woman had typed up all the lectures I had given since I came back from India and handed me a huge stack of papers, which I drove out to Lama with. When I got there, all the people living there spread everything out on low tables, and took different parts of it to illustrate. It was really a cocreated, wild experiment because nobody had ever created a book like that.

The concept BE HERE NOW, explores what it means to be fully present. In learning how to be fully present, I began to let the past go with forgiveness and let the future go without anticipation. I discovered that when I'm not dwelling in the past or anticipating the future I could just be right here, right now. We're outside of time. THIS IS IT!! This is all there is. RIGHT NOW! Later never exists. Here we are. Here and now. That's all there is. We finally figure out that it's only the clock that's going around. It's doing its thing, but you, you're sitting HERE RIGHT NOW, always.

Free yourself from the illusion of good and bad days. Labeling time makes us nostalgic of the past and demanding of the future. There is only here and now. Let it be.

Much of spiritual work is slowing down enough to let our minds come into harmony with our hearts. I believe that when you go inside to your spiritual heart, to your God within, there you will find loving awareness and your inner strength. The past, for everybody, is thoughts. And the future is thoughts. And the worst thing is dwelling in thoughts, in the mind. Dwelling in the heart is better; being present in the moment. This is how I've practiced being here now.

Practicing being here now helped me to stand back enough to see the pieces of my life and see what I was really working on. I could look at it all with awareness and think, "Am I creating a life that is fulfilling my unique opportunities in the universe? Am I understanding the life I'm creating as part of my spiritual path? What do I want to phase out, what do I want to keep?" I stood back and got a feeling of the design of my life. And once I was at peace with the design of my life, then when I was at each thing, I could fully be in the thing I was in, present in each moment.

Serve Everyone

When I was in India, Maharajji gave me the name Ram Dass, and I said, "Is it good?" And they said, "Yeah. RAM (rhymes with mom) is God and DASS (rhymes with boss) is servant. Servant of God." Well, despite my curiosities, I didn't have one whiff of God until I took psychedelics, so I wanted to better understand how I could live up to this new name.

As I understood it, there are many kinds of practices or routes up the mountain, or routes that extricate yourself from your ego, and connect you with your soul, and some are more attractive to one person than another. The interesting thing is they all lead to the top. I was very attracted to Buddhism because it had a lot of that, and so did a lot of various mystic traditions. I was also drawn to hatha yoga because I was interested in the energies of the body and the spirit. I had somewhat of an aversion to the physical, psychological, social plane, and I was not attracted to a form of yoga that would involve me so much with the world around me. I thought in order to live more from my soul, I needed to seek out esoteric, secret spiritual teachings and initiations, climb a secret mountain, meditate in a cave, then have a special mantra whispered to me, and do holy things. I thought this was what was needed to change my whole spiritual life and help me connect to my soul. Is this what you're thinking will change your whole spiritual life? That's what I was waiting for. What I got instead was this old guy in a blanket.

I waited until I was alone with Maharajji and I said, "Maharajji, how can I know God?" And he said, "Feed people." That was such a weird answer that I assumed the translator screwed up. I mean that's hardly the secret teaching I was thinking would change my whole spiritual life. So I figured I'd rephrase it: "Maharajji, how can I get enlightened?" And he said, "Serve people. Feed people and serve people." So I thought, "What does he know??" But the problem was, I knew he knew, and I just didn't want to do it. So I did everything else instead until I came back around to what he'd told me.

After I received my name, I was listening for how I would live up to the name meaning 'servant of God'. One day I was sitting in meditation, and I began to hear, "Your way, your lineage, has to do with your name, Ram Dass, which means servant of God, which is part of the lineage of the Hindu monkey Hanuman. It has to do with service." Maharajji said, "Remember God. Remember God. Whatever you do, remember God. Remember God." And then he pointed to Hanuman and told stories about Hanuman. Most people thought that Maharajji was Hanuman. And Hanuman was serving God. That is the image I came back from India with. And what Maharajji was saying to me during my meditation was, "Your route through is service." "You can meditate; it'll quiet your mind. It'll deepen your appreciation and awareness, and it's wonderful. Meditation is very useful," he used to say, but my primary route to connect with my soul and God was going to be through service. So what I tried to figure out for a few years was how service could be a method of serving God, and contributing to the relief of suffering. Maharajji gave instructions to love everybody, serve, and remember. And I worked to do just that.

My path up the mountain, since I had a yearning to serve and relieve suffering, was called the path of action, or in the Eastern way, KARMA YOGA. This would become my inner work of contemplation and my outer work of action. The inner, meditative work would help me to do my service work in the outer world with equanimity, wisdom, love and presence. Doing my work in the outer world helped me to practice contemplation in action, by using service as a method to bring me inward while I do outer work. It was like a self-sharpening tool because as I was serving I was also noticing that service was a process of working on myself. Gradually I became clearer, quieter, and more present. I was able to listen more deeply and able to serve better. My route up the mountain became karma yoga, of love and service. It's just another route through. It's a very beautiful way, but it's only another path.

I wanted my life to be a statement of love and compassion. I realized I wanted to move toward those things that most people looked away from. So a few of the things I did to get started on the path of service were to support the dying, to work with people who were incarcerated in prisons, and I joined with others to end preventable blindness. SEVA is the Sanskrit word for selfless service, or service to God. For me, service and social action were my methods for coming closer

In the Hindu epic the RAMAYANA, Ram, another form of God, asks Hanuman the monkey, "Who are you?" Hanuman says, "When I don't know who I am, I serve you. When I do know who I am, I am you."

to God. I was listening to how I could serve God in every human being. My life became a dialogue with God. This dialogue was a great support to me, especially at first when I found the suffering to be so immense.

There is such an ocean of suffering in the world. There's also pleasure and beauty and fun and play and an ocean of love, but there is also suffering. There is suffering of every conceivable kind, and often people isolate themselves from the suffering of others. What I experienced is that the ocean of suffering is so vast, and the media brings it so immediately to you, the faces of the people around you and the stories about other cultures. When you look at the news, it is so filled with crisis, and pain, and terror, and deceit, and greed, and lust. It's so intense that what often happens is you feel powerless before this ocean, this wave, this tidal wave of suffering. I know at first I did.

And the truth is, we are part of a community. We are part of a social, political, and economic community. We might often wish we weren't a part of it, but we are. Really though, it is only US. There's no THEM. If you try to hold onto a THEM you close your heart. You armor your heart. It's like our hearts are all connected in the universe, like pebble drops rippling through the water.

ALL ONE

You know, I think the heart is the only institution that I trust as an agent for social change. It's not the big organization, not the government, not the family. It comes down to one human heart seeing another, to another, to another, to another. That's social change. That's the way I define social action, as heart to heart to heart. You love completely and with your heart open and you love everybody, as a soul, completely. With a deep and real compassion. Not pity and not sort of social kindness, but real kindness that comes out of deep, deep compassion, and you take care of the environment, not because I'm going to sacrifice for the environment, but because I am the environment, and I hurt. Now as we face the ecological issues of the times, the political issues of the times, change and potential chaos, we have the opportunity to join the people that have already dealt with that chaos of mind to lend this culture strength and equanimity in the face of suffering and uncertainty.

I would say that one of our biggest obstacles in the area of service is inertia, our tendency to be passive and do nothing. People know in their hearts that they would like to reach out to another human being and help, but they fear they don't have the skills, or they're paranoid that they'll be taken advantage of, or they're frightened that once it starts they won't be able to stop. They end up holding back. That's the hardest obstacle, overcoming that initial inertia. Once you're into it, once you've done it, it becomes much easier. The first time is a little tricky.

There are other mindsets that prevent us from taking action. For example, you're part of a government, whether you like it or not, and not voting is voting. If you're saying, "I'm not having anything to do with politics because it's too dirty and because I don't approve of it," then forget it. You are abdicating or rejecting your responsibility to society. It's as simple as that. I think we're at an interesting moment within the shift of collective consciousness, specifically around the way in which we're integrating the changes in power structures. How is the shift in collective consciousness going to evolve, and what part do you play?

We're all a little broken and a little shattered inside. Each of us is aspiring to make it to the end. None is deprived of pain here and we have all suffered in our own ways. I think our journey is all about healing

ourselves and healing
each other in our own
special ways. Let's just
help each other put
all those pieces back
together and make it to
the end more beautifully.
Let us help each
other survive.

Part of the curriculum of life is looking at the systems that you are a part of and being able to say, "That system needs work." It's important to be able to shift your game so that you're not simply pushing the system away and saying, "I don't think about that stuff because it's too complicated. Let somebody else worry about it." Honestly, your inaction may be standing in the way of everybody's survival. Since we must act, we do the best we can to act consciously and compassionately. But in addition, we can make every action an exercise designed to help us become free. Because the truth that comes from freedom, and the power that comes from freedom, and the love and compassion that come from freedom are the jewels we can cultivate to offer to our fellow sentient beings for the relief of their suffering.

Even though we find ourselves afraid, and not feeling peaceful, and less than fully loving and compassionate, we must act. There is no way you can be in an incarnation without acting. We cannot wait until we are enlightened to act in the world, and we don't need to withdraw from the world to become enlightened. We all hear the way in which our silence is itself an act of acquiescence to a system, which allows the status quo to continue. I think it's very hard to understand, when it seems like our participation is such a trivial act, how it's connected to the entire universe that way, but I feel that it's important not only for the relief of suffering that you do what you can for other people, but it's also important for your own heart that you do something.

Like I've mentioned before, I can disagree with a political leader's actions. I can lobby for legislative changes. I can protest if I think what they support is wrong. I can disagree with actions that are not compassionate. But I want to keep my heart open. If I don't, I am part of the problem, not part of the solution. That's what the inner work is, to become part of the solution. You don't have to act out of anger in order to oppose something because it creates suffering. You can become an instrument of that which relieves suffering by opposing somebody with love. You can do social action out of love.

We cannot really presume to know the final meaning of our actions. Nevertheless, we should work full-time to end suffering, having no attachment to whether suffering ends. There came a point when I said, "I'll just do what I can. I'll do what I can to relieve suffering. I'll do what I can to preserve the environment, sustainably. I'll do what I can to bring about justice in the world." I think it's important that at some level we care with all our heart, and then we finally let go. We give it all we have, and trust the rest to God, to nature, to the universe. You might ask, "How can you know you're not making errors that are increasing suffering when you work to relieve suffering?" The answer is you don't, and all you can do is stay open with your heart and your mind and be as impeccable as you know how to be, and be willing to admit you've blown it and made errors.

None of us are so naive as to think that only that which gives pleasure is useful. I think most of you now have found through your own experiences that there is incredible growth through suffering. That doesn't mean that we would go around programming suffering into people's lives. We don't teach Suffering 101. And yes, when we look back at our own lives we see that some of the most profound changes occurred at the times of the most intense suffering. Little did I know how valuable this wisdom would be for me in the next chapter of my life.

Stroked

I was a very independent person, kind of self-involved. I was galumphing through life before the stroke and I kind of thought that was all there was. And then one evening I was lying in bed about to fall asleep, imagining what it must be like to be a very old man. I was writing a book about aging, and I was thinking about how the book should end.

And then my life drastically changed for the third time. It took some time for me to comprehend that I had a massive cerebral hemorrhage, a near fatal stroke that brought me very close to death.

I was told I had only a ten percent chance of survival. The doctors were saying, "He's going to die," and they all looked at me with these long faces and I didn't have the faintest idea that I was dying. I mean, me, Mr. Spiritual, except all I was doing was studying the pipes on the ceiling. I had spent so many hours sitting by the bedside of the dying, thinking spiritual thoughts, and I assumed the dying person was also thinking spiritual thoughts. So I thought when my time came that I, too, would be thinking spiritual thoughts. What's interesting is that I, Mr. Spiritual, didn't have one spiritual thought and in my own death I didn't orient toward the spirit. It showed me I have some work to do because I thought, "That's the test." So I thought I'd flunked the test.

I looked around the hospital and all these doctors, nurses, my family, my friends, they were all, "Tsk, tsk, tsk, tsk." "You had a stroke." "You poor thing." "Ah, too bad you've had a stroke." "Oh, that's too bad you're stroked." There was a time when I bought into everybody else's mind. They thought, "Poor Ram Dass." And I said, "Poor Ram Dass."

Their minds were rubbing off on me, so I felt this was a terrible terrible thing that happened, and it was unexpected and stuff like that. One thing that was hard to get through, in the stroke, was other peoples' minds, because they were reacting to the incarnation, and the body. My awareness wasn't affected by the stroke, but my body was.

When I was in India, I met my guru who was a very spiritually powerful person, and I felt I was under his wing and that I was therefore graced. I thought that he would never let anything unfortunate happen to me. The stroke changed that position. After the stroke, I thought, "Maharajji?!" "What the hell?!" "Did you go out to lunch?" I mean, "Look at this!" "I'm a strokee!" Because, "How did this happen to me?!" "How could he do this to me?!"

After the stroke, I got pretty depressed for several months. I had three reasons. First, I was in a lot of physical pain. Second, I was in psychological shock, because I, who was independent, was now dependent. I was this independent person, and now I had to call somebody to get out of bed. The third suffering was the spiritual one, the spiritual suffering. The third one was the fact that I had fallen out of grace. That stung me, you know. Because up until then, I had led a graced life. The stroke affected my faith. Because I just, you know, I had a lack of faith. I missed it. And without faith, you feel nothing. When you have faith, you feel grace. Grace to me is help from a beneficent universe. You feel it, you feel it like snow, you feel it like it surrounds you. It colors your life. It spiritualizes your life; that's what grace does.

The stroke didn't look like grace to me. So I thought I was at the end of a graced life. And everybody said, "Are you depressed about your stroke?" I said, "No, I don't care about my stroke, I care about my faith." Belief is up here in the mind and faith is down here in the heart. I had negative thoughts in my mind, and there were very negative feelings in me because I realized I was missing my faith. The stroke had taken my faith in Maharajji. The stroke caused me to lose faith, and it was a cold, cold place, and when that passed, I realized it was fierce grace.

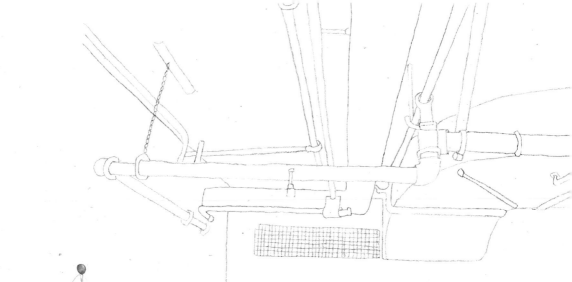

FIERCE GRACE was what I called it, because it was a grace that turned my life around. Because the stroke took my world and shook it upside down. The stroke upset all my plans. But I didn't say, "F@%k you, God!" "You got a hell of a nerve!" "That's not part of my plan!" I didn't want to complain and say that, "If I were God, I would have done it differently!" because that would bring my consciousness in opposition to God. And I don't want to do that, because the judging mind is rough stuff.

Someone hung a picture of Maharajji on the wall in my hospital room. I would stare at it. It told me to meditate, to go inward instead of outward. And he smiled in the picture and he said to me, "Just wait. Just wait." "Wait and see. Wait and see."

In the hospital, I used to sit in my bed and continuously think about how the stroke could be grace, but I struggled to see it that way. Everyday in the hospital I gave myself a spiritual exercise. I started each day cataloging how the stroke was a benefit.

This new practice created a belief system so strong that it helped me take what could be called a sad tune and turn it into a happy tune. It changed the entire meaning of the situation. Spirit connected with my rehabilitation, and I finally broke through the negative attitudes and judging toward the stroke. I thought it seemed like very awful grace for my ego but might have a benefit for my soul. I talked to my guru inside, and I finally saw that it was grace. I came to see the terrible situation I got into as grace because I learned something about suffering and love from it. Maybe you can relate?

What brought me out of my depression was when I stopped looking outside myself for happiness. I started looking inside and started to feel joy. This too was grace. From that point on I felt my soul. I was feeling the soul's perception that everything was lovable and the whole universe was giving me love.

The stroke wasn't grace. The stroke was from nature. I was learning that the stroke itself was not grace but my reactions to the stroke were grace. I was positive from it, I was fascinated by it, and it was changing my philosophy on life.

Meeting Between the Words

I saw the stroke as a new chapter in the life of this body. It's very interesting to me because it's so uniquely different than the last chapter. I had this new identity to explore, which was that of a wheelchair-bound person. I really explored what it means not to have the same power that I used to.

The stroke was like a whole new incarnation. I know this isn't who I expected to be. But, you know, I was okay. No, don't feel sorry for me, because that's just wasting your time to feel sorry. It was just a new stage of life.

In my previous chapters I could speak. At the beginning of this chapter, I was mostly silent, with long pauses in my speech. The stroke left my right side pretty much paralyzed, and it cut many things out of my life. The stroke kept me from doing my favorite things and took away my external pleasures. They were all wiped out, so I saw this as the perfect time for meditating. It's as if God gave me a little message saying, "Don't you think it's time you looked even deeper inside?" Many of us get so consumed in the outside world that we don't take the opportunity to look deep within until someone gets sick or a family member or friend gets sick, or something like that.

The stroke had an interesting effect. All of the pain, the psychological pain, the spiritual pain, and the physical pain, forced me to go somewhere else. It pushed me into my soul, into a different plane of consciousness. The stroke forced me to become the witness, and from my soul's perspective I could observe the pain, these thoughts, this ego and this incarnation. I found it much less painful to watch than to experience. I went from identifying with my ego to identifying with my soul, my spiritual identity. Now, it doesn't take a stroke to move from ego to soul, but it certainly helped me to take the perspective of the witness, which is part of the soul, and the soul loves everything. I got so identified with my soul that I saw my whole incarnation as love. There are qualities in me that never would have come out. Never. I became more at peace than I have ever been. The peace came from my settling into the moment and not dwelling in thoughts of the past or fears about the future.

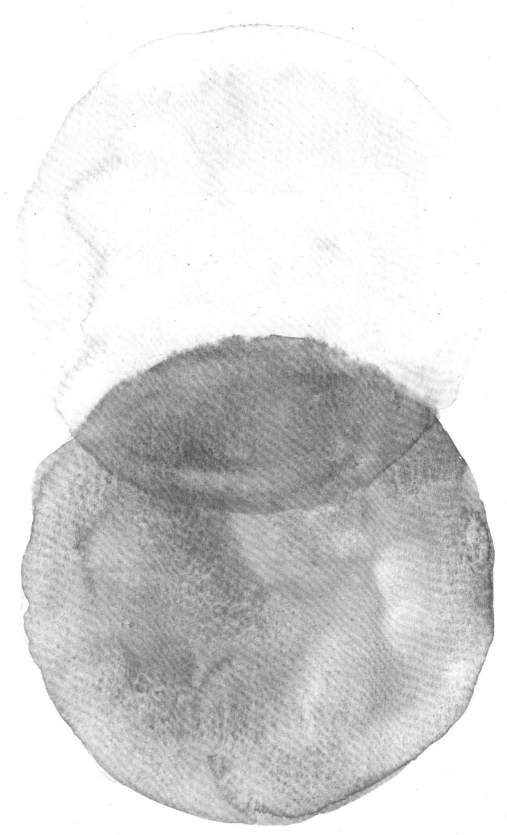

The stroke allowed me to settle into silence, and it turned out to be a gift in many ways. I no longer needed to impress people or be clever or profound or entertaining. My god, I could barely talk. I got over most of it, but I had to deal with silence and that was a great benefit spiritually. Even while I struggled to speak during my lectures, I saw how the silence brought us closer to one another and to God. So I incorporated silent pauses into speeches, and the nature of my work shifted to emphasize the spaces between the words rather than the words themselves. The stroke gave me another way to serve people. It let me feel more deeply the pain of others; to help them know, by example, that ultimately whatever happens, no harm can come.

Surf the silences with me. The silences allow for a deeper connection. It's a place where words were left far behind. Where our mind doesn't get in the way, and our hearts know one another. To me, this is a model of what human relationships can be.

Change is an opportunity for growth, and it requires an openness to the unknown. You and I are in training to be stable in the presence of change, not holding onto the old system, but being able to move into the unknown without fear. We are in training to find a place in ourselves, and in the way we live our lives, where we don't freak out about changes, where we don't freak out in the presence of change or increasing chaos.

It's going to be at that moment of chaos when those people who have some tiny degree of equanimity and balance will be the thing around which we can coalesce in a stable shift that is healing, instead of one that ultimately ends in destruction. It's scaring the hell out of most of us because the changes that are occurring are so fast and rapid and unpredictable and on the edge of chaos. I think the best advice for dealing with unpredictable change is to expect nothing, to take every experience, including the negative ones, as merely steps on the path, and to proceed. It's as simple as that. Honor it, love it, don't judge it, just allow it.

Give it space. Give the universe space.

Allowing this helped me realize that the universe changes from inside, to see the higher wisdom in this, and not be frightened or trapped by the concept of change.

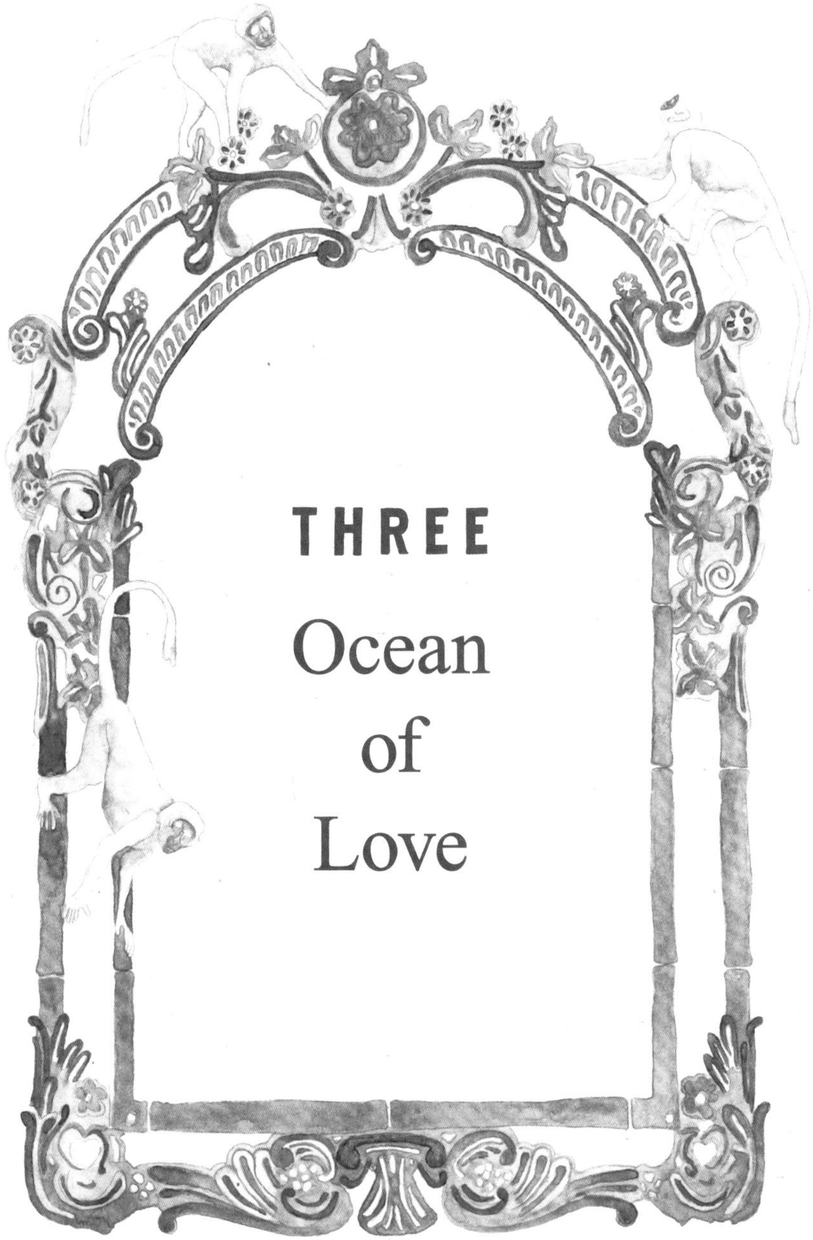

THREE
Ocean of Love

I Am Loving Awareness

After the stroke I accepted the fact that my life changed and things would be different, although I still got a lot of invitations to play the old Ram Dass. I was just happy watching the sun change positions over the Pacific Ocean because what I really wanted to do most is sit and meditate. But my main spiritual practice was not meditation so much as talking to Maharajji, which is like talking to my higher self, a conversation of the heart.

I was really content. Maui was a refuge for me. Most of my adult life was going from city to city on speaking tours. This was a good place to stop and do my spiritual work. I have so much gratitude for living on Maui, but that wasn't what made me content.

When I looked back at my life, twenty-five years ago, thirty years ago, forty years ago, who I became would hardly recognize who I was back then. And who I became felt great compassion for who I was then. And who I am now feels great compassion for who he was then. When I was young, my personality was so real and I was so closely identified with it that it was very hard to change. As the context broadened, I invested less energy in my personality, and it became easier for me to change. Life actually became fun. That wasn't something I could say back in my teens and twenties. I wasn't having fun back then because I was so concerned about achieving something and always afraid of failing. I was also constantly worried about whether people were going to like me. Some of that had dissipated by the time I was fifty, but the stroke cut through the last of my attachments to striving. I stopped comparing with the past. Those days were over.

You and I will find that as we go on this journey we are less and less definable. I've learned, from going through so many transformations of who I know myself to be and how it is, that I must assume that those will continue. There's no reason to assume they won't, although they may not.

Now I identify with being loving awareness, with consciousness, which is the One. I think it gets easier and easier to identify with the soul and come from the heart, because as you're aging, you're looking at everything from a distance and you're more peaceful and loving. I was content with my aging body. I was free and happy, in love with everyone and everything. I saw the beauty of the universe, including my aging body. I was getting peaceful, and identifying with that peacefulness within me. I could just sit there and let consciousness play, enjoy the scenery and the visitors. My consciousness had withdrawn from worldly things and could prepare for death and fully meditate on loving awareness.

I live in love.

The trees are love,

the clouds are love.

They are made of love,

because they are

manifestations of the One.

Like nature.

We are nature too.

I perceive myself and

the universe as love.
The universe is an example
of love. Like a tree.
Like my body.
Like my wheelchair.
I see the love. And
I'm immersed in the
ocean of love.

We have to get out of our thinking minds. I'll tell you how I do it, by using a mantra, a phrase. I'll give you a mantra. Concentrate on your spiritual heart, right in the middle of your chest, on the heart-mind. I may take a few deep breaths into my diaphragm to help me identify with it. I breathe in love, and breathe out love. I watch all of the thoughts that create the stuff of my mind, and I love everything, love everything I can be aware of. Now, keep repeating the phrase, "I am loving awareness."

"I am loving awareness. I am loving a
I am loving awareness. I am lovi
I am loving awareness. I am l
I am loving awareness." Yc

ness. I am loving awareness.

wareness. I am loving awareness.

g awareness. I am loving awareness.

g awareness. I am loving awareness.

e loving awareness. YOU ARE A SOUL.

I think life can
be preparation
for death, so we might
as well get ready for the
change and aim for a death in
which we are fully present in the
moment. Bye-bye incarnation. Present
in the moment. Present in the moment.
That's the key in death. That's the key
in life. Present in the moment. Present in
the moment. Giving up measures of where you
are in the process, so giving up time, giving up
space. Surrender, surrender, surrender.

Death is the biggest change we'll face. I thought a lot about
my own death and was concentrating on what happens after that.
It was part of my spiritual practice. I knew a time would come
when I'd say, "Alright, now I'm ready." In the meantime I thought

THE BEST THING I COULD DO TO PREPARE FOR MY
DEATH IS TO OPEN MY HEART, QUIET MY MIND, LET GO
OF MY EXPECTATIONS, AND WHILE I'M WAITING DO WHAT
I CAN TO RELIEVE SUFFERING.

Which was also my approach to life. I'd say that, perhaps mostly death is really just completely surrendering to the moment. That's it. When contemplating death I think it's common for most of us to feel our minds thinking its way out of it. "But what about the past?" "But what about the future?" "But what about the children?" "But my family?" "But? But? But?"

I think we have a great deal to learn about the dignity of the processes of life and death, and understanding them in a way to release us rather than to torment us. This requires a different kind of a perceptual view of the universe than we are used to. Because in many cultures, although death has come out of the closet, it is still not openly experienced or discussed. The more I've allowed death to be present in my consciousness, I've noticed that the moment is filled with added preciousness, joy and energy that otherwise is used up in denial.

I encourage you to make peace with death, to see it as the culmination of this adventure called life. It is not an error. It is not a failure. It's taking off a tight shoe, which you have worn well. We want to open to death as part of life, to embrace death truly and hold it gently. To be able to do that is extraordinary. For me, appreciating death and the spiritual journey after death has given my life its fullness of meaning, which is to see death as part of life.

I think you'd agree that death is one of the greatest mysteries and a moment of incredible transformation. Contemplating death has been such a gift for me. It just keeps me right at the edge of mystery. So I thought about it, and I thought, well, "I want to approach this mystery with a sense of adventure and a clear mind, with an appreciation and love for the mystery and the form of the universe. I would like to be present at that moment. If death is just around the corner, I want to get comfortable in the role of being a listener to the mystery."

Ultimate Frontier

Dying is the great frontier for every one of us. I can guarantee that every-body in the world is going to die one day. I can see it with my mystic powers! Now, you're either going to freak about it, or you're going to say, "Well, won't that be interesting?!" And you're going to live this moment, and this moment, and this moment. And one of these moments will be the moment that you will drop your body.

I'm one of those unusual types who enjoys being with someone when they're dying. And what I learned from sitting with people who are dying is that I know I'm going to be in the presence of truth. And after they take their last breath, I know that their ceremony is only half done because the soul comes into death from this plane and then continues on. I'm not a medical doctor, a nurse, a lawyer, or an ordained priest. But what I could offer to another human being is the presence of a sacred, spacious environment. And I offered them love. Because I identified with my own soul, I could see their soul and say, "I'm going to be neutral. And if you want a neutral, loving rock, I'm here." But I had to work with my fear about death to be able to offer a spaciousness so they have the opportunity to die as they need to die.

It seems that there are several fears when confronting death. Some people are anxious about the pain of dying; others are afraid of the moment of death, fearing that it will be a horrible moment, like a bad acid trip, and some people are anxious about what happens after death. When it's your natural time to go, if you approach death as a transition for the soul then there is nothing to be scared about. Well, you want to be scared; the pain and that stuff, that's to be scared about. But the dying part, there's nothing to be scared of. The soul is not afraid of death because it has done birth and death and birth and death infinitely. As a soul, you see yourselves as reincarnations. As a soul, I have no fear.

I took my last few breaths, and then totally surrendered to death on December 22, 2019, as the light began to return on the winter solstice and the first night of Chanukah. It was my wish that my body stay in the house for a few days so my friends and satsang could come over and visit, and that's actually what happened. My caregivers washed and dressed me and laid me out on a table surrounded by fresh roses. People came by to say goodbye to my body, and chanted prayers to Hanuman. It was beautiful. My body was cremated on the last day of the decade, December 31, 2019.

Each time we form an attachment to another human being it is, of course, inevitable that sooner or later one of you is going to die. So in a way, the nature of attachment to human beings has loss built in. That's part of what makes life

The soul functions in love, and love transcends death.

precious and frightening at the same moment. The prospect of loss is what actually intensifies the attachment. The attachment contains the recognition, at some level, that everything is uncertain and changing all the time. Many of us have felt the fear of loving too much, the fear and pain of loving when you know there will be a loss. And when there is a loss, there is of course deep grief. And the way we deal with grief has a lot to do with whether or not the grief heals and strengthens us or ends up depriving and starving us.

I suspect that after the loss of the physical presence of our loved ones burns its way through, and you deal with the desolation, and the grief, and the sense of separateness, and you can quiet down just a bit and listen very carefully and just sit with it, you will start to feel in your heart a very deep and profound loving connection that is very living. This connection is not just a memory, it's a living truth. And that will start to nurture you.

My guru, who is the closest being that I've ever had
in my life, closer than my parents or any lover,
left his body in 1973, but remained a living truth
that I lived with every day. And the fact
that he wasn't in his form just makes
me understand him in ways much more
profoundly than I ever would have had
he remained in his form. When someone
you love dies, the trueness of the love
that is shared remains. And when you
loved somebody enough to miss them, you
knew them in a way in which that was true
conscious love. But we get so attached to
our senses and thoughts about a person as
an object that we feel we lose something when
they die. And when we quiet down, we realize that the
relationship just moved to a new level of richness, a new
way of being together.

If a person comes to me who has had a loved one die, I say
to the person, "Go light a candle and talk to your beloved."
And they say, "Well, do they talk back?" And I say, "Well that
depends. I've been talking to my guru and he died in 1973.
So, I guess." They say, "C'mon you're imagining things!" I say,
"That's right!" Because I believe that It's through the
imagination where we can communicate with souls. Words,
feelings and presence is all that's needed.

This lifetime is an incarnation, and we get so identified with this life and our egos that it's hard to remember past lives. Most of us have no memory of our previous incarnations. Nature shows us the cycle of life. Death. Life. Death. Life. Death.

We are on that cycle too. I know this all may sound ridiculous, and of course I can't say for certain, except that I intuitively feel that reincarnation is right. Accepting this helped me look at my incarnation and ask, "What have I learned?" I learned about suffering and I learned about love. These are the things I really learned in my heart and down in my bones. I believe that you, as a soul, have also taken this incarnation to learn something about suffering and about love.

Each of us contains a soul that doesn't die and an ego that does die.

Everything must change except the soul.

Identify with your soul now.

Identify with your soul now.

Identify with your soul now.

Your death from this
incarnation is like the
end of a chapter of a
book. It's that fast.
Dying is the most
important moment
that exists in any
incarnation.

It's important
that you not be so
overwhelmed by the
processes of time.

I wish you a process for dying
that doesn't overwhelm you. I
wish you a moment of time that
you can be conscious of. I wish you to
be in a plane of incredible light.

Soul Pod

There are realms, or planes of consciousness, other than the one we meet on. Sensual planes. Planes with color, music. Planes that have no form.

In life, these other planes of consciousness can be accessible through various methods, like dreaming, meditation, chanting, and others, but they are also accessed after death. I can't prove it for certain, but I believe that when the body and ego die, they die into soul, completely identified as an individual soul, and into the next plane of consciousness. Here, you can look around for a veil, or a doorway that takes you to this next plane of consciousness.

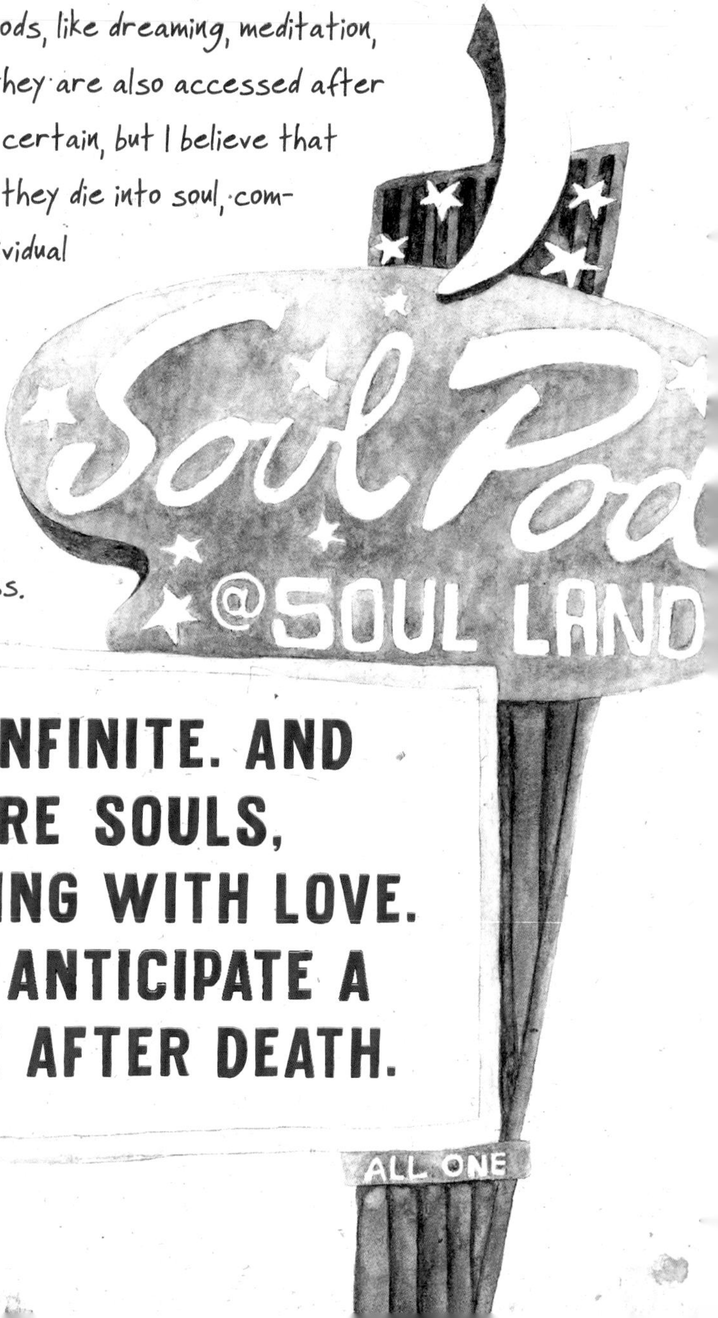
Soul Pod
@SOUL LAND
ALL ONE

SOULS ARE INFINITE. AND SINCE THEY'RE SOULS, THEY'RE LIVING WITH LOVE. SO YOU CAN ANTICIPATE A LOVING TIME AFTER DEATH.

I see that death is the last spiritual practice. After that, we continue being souls. Being in the One. Being love. Being all these trees. Being the wind. Being the universe. You will come through the doorway to a much different kind of identity than the one on which you have been functioning from the time of birth, and which was transmitted through those who trained you to be somebody.

This is a realm where we meet the souls we have known in the past. As just souls. We won't meet them in their clothing or role of mother or father, or uncle or aunt, or friend. There are things I call SOUL PODS. These are just familiar souls who hang out and travel together and are connected in consciousness. Just like satsang, it's a loving community of souls, your spiritual family, that is accessible for you in life and after death. You meet these familiar souls in this plane of consciousness that I call SOUL LAND. It's great to be in Soul Land. Here, time is relative. Soul Land has no time, no space. In Soul Land, you meet your soul pod that has been with you infinitely. Your soul pod has been travel- ing with you since it all began. The soul pod asks what you learned from your incarnation, just like your satsang does.

In Soul Land you'll find another doorway, and then another plane. This next plane is where all of it starts. It's sometimes explained as the womb, the beginning of things. This plane is ecstatic. It's the ultimate creativity.

In Soul Land you come through this doorway, and the minute we go up into this higher plane of consciousness, we are in the One.

This is the plane of God, the plane of consciousness, the plane of awareness.

Here, as a soul, one comes to the essence.

The One.

You perceive the One.
The ocean of love.
And consciousness.

God and your guru.

Now we're dealing with the place where when you know yourself as that, you just are. Here, there is no time anymore. You are going nowhere and you're coming from nowhere.

Eventually, in some incarnation, when we've finished our work our soul can merge back into the One, back into God, back into the infinite. In the meantime, as I've said before, our soul is using bodies, egos and personalities to work through the karma of each incarnation.

Have I taken birth before? I have no experiential knowledge of that, but from where I am sitting, undoubtedly thousands and thousands of times. Will I take birth again? Undoubtedly, thousands and thousands of times. My body lived for eighty-eight years, feeling aches and pains, desires and emotions, passions of life, the hatreds and the joys. But me, I'm in here and I'm... infinite. MY SOUL IS INFINITE. My soul is filled with so much love.

Time passes, things change.

And with awakening, one begins to see the way one has been trapped in one's storyline. But it doesn't mean the story ends. The Ram Dass story is alive and well. The only question is who's living it.

I love you.
And my love is
a spiritual love.
It's unconditional
love.

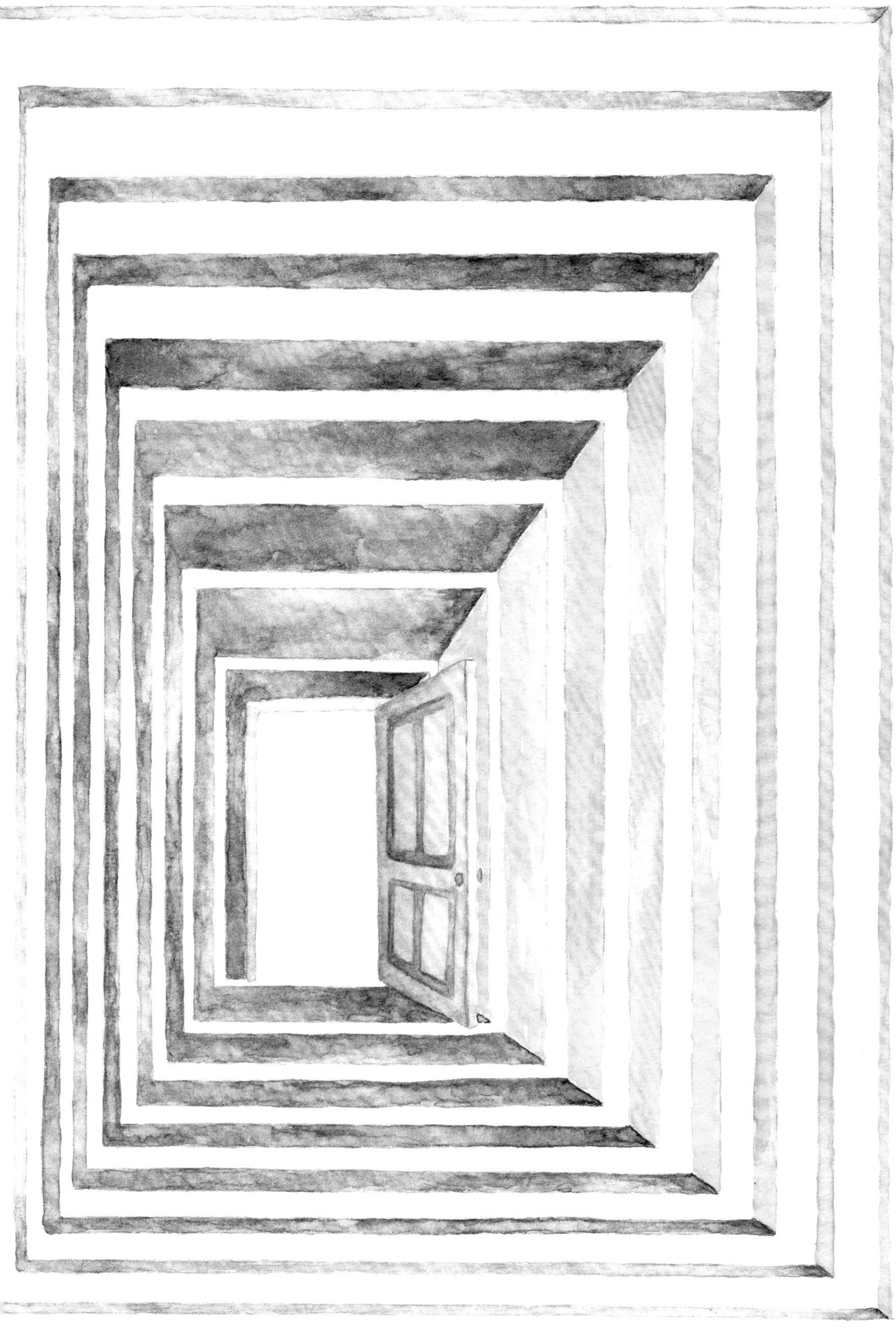

HER

HERE

HERE

HERE

FROM HERE TO HERE, TO HERE

HERE

HERE

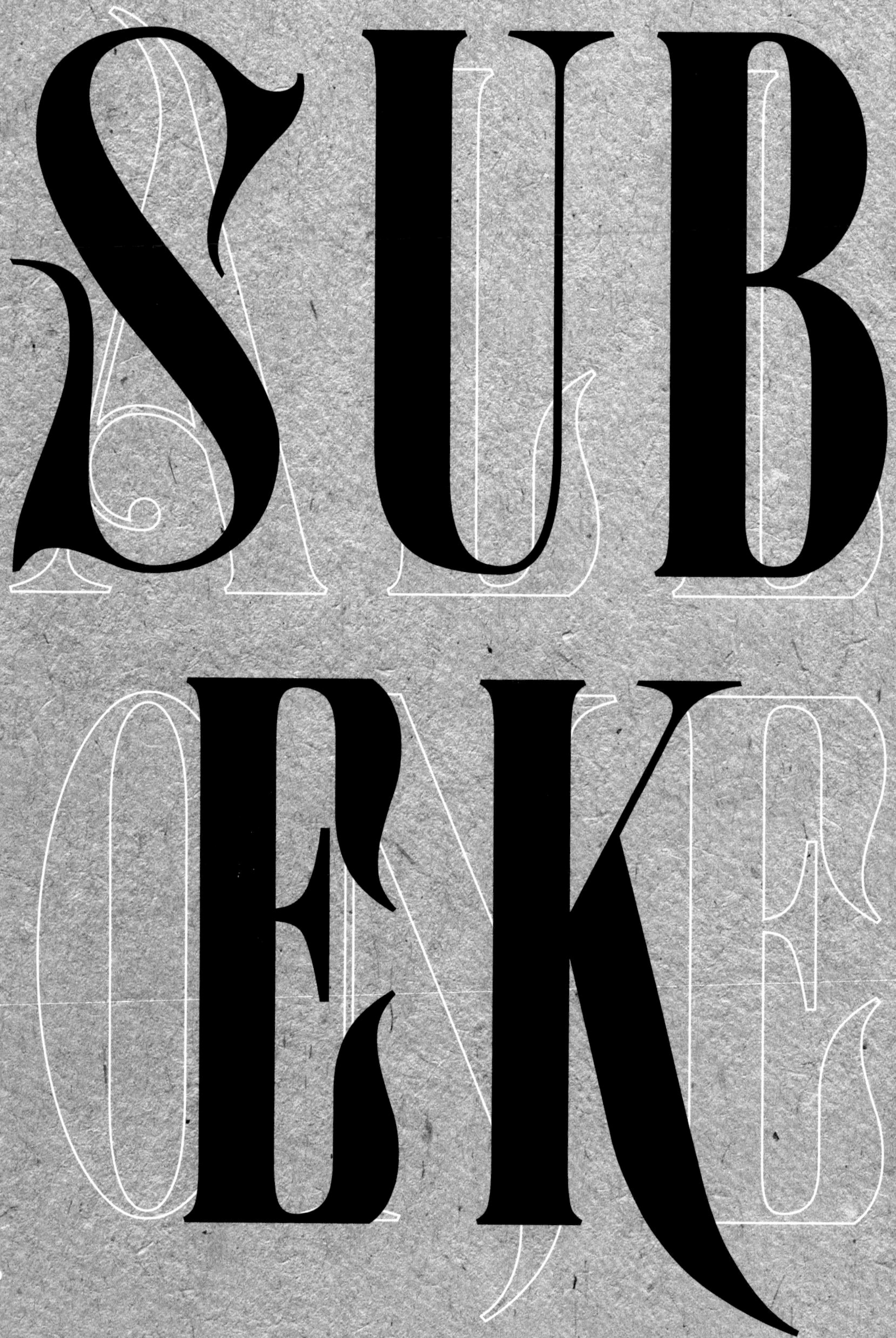

SUB
EKC

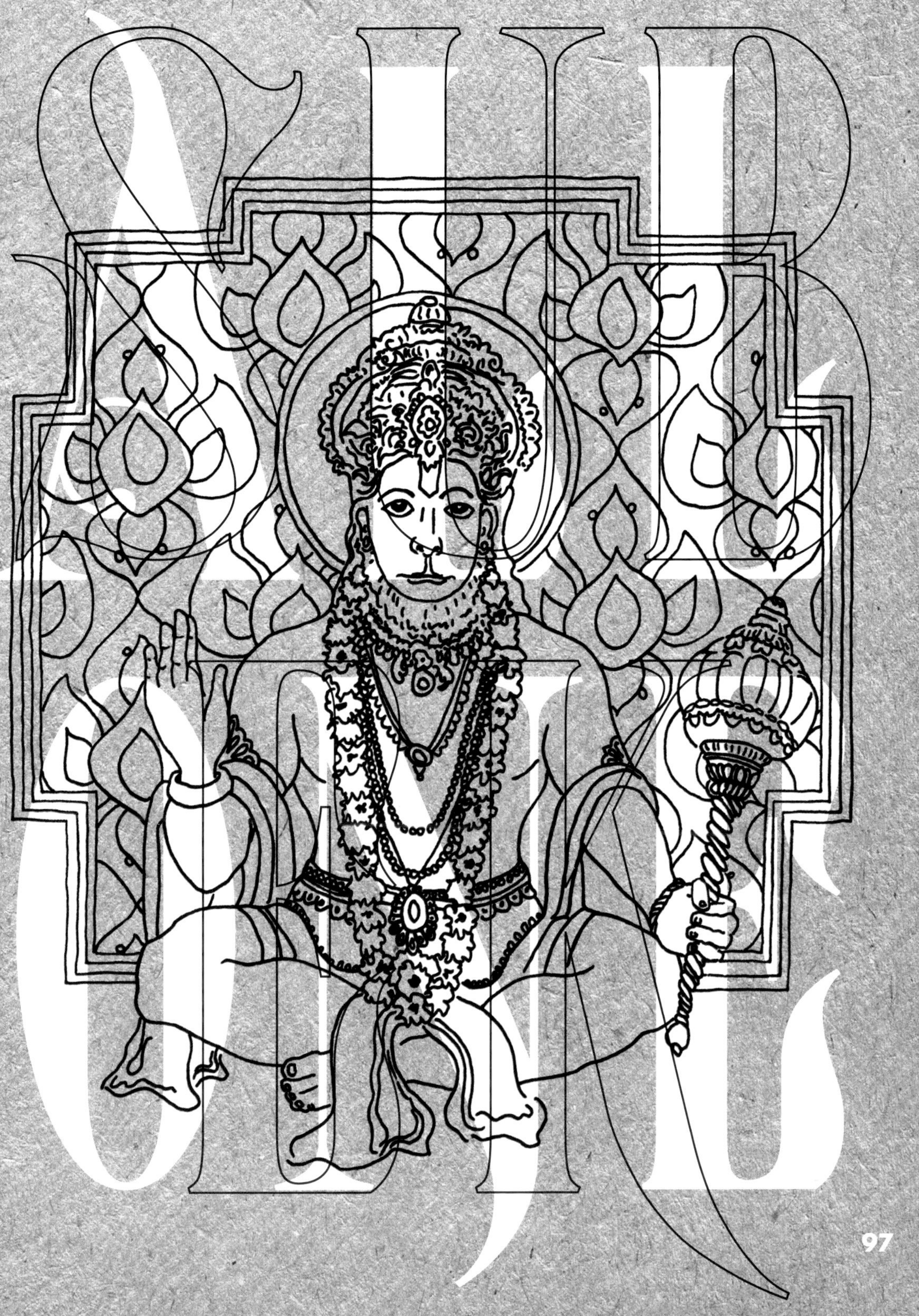

THE WORK YOU'RE DOING BECOMES- YOUR

START FROM WHERE YOU ARE, NOT WHERE

PATH.

YOU WISH
YOU WERE.

FINDING OUR TRUE SELF IS A LIFELONG SEARCH.

IT'S NOT CALLED PRACTICE FOR NOTHING. YOU ACTUALLY HAVE TO TREAD ON THE PATH TO GET SOMEWHERE. NOT THAT THERE'S ANYWHERE TO GO; IT'S JUST ABOUT BECOMING MORE HERE, MORE PRESENT IN THIS MOMENT. ONCE WE BEGIN TO EXPLORE OUR OWN PSYCHE, MIND AND HEART, WE BEGIN TO APPRECIATE THAT EVERYBODY ELSE IS IN THE SAME SITUATION. WE'RE NOT SO DIFFERENT.

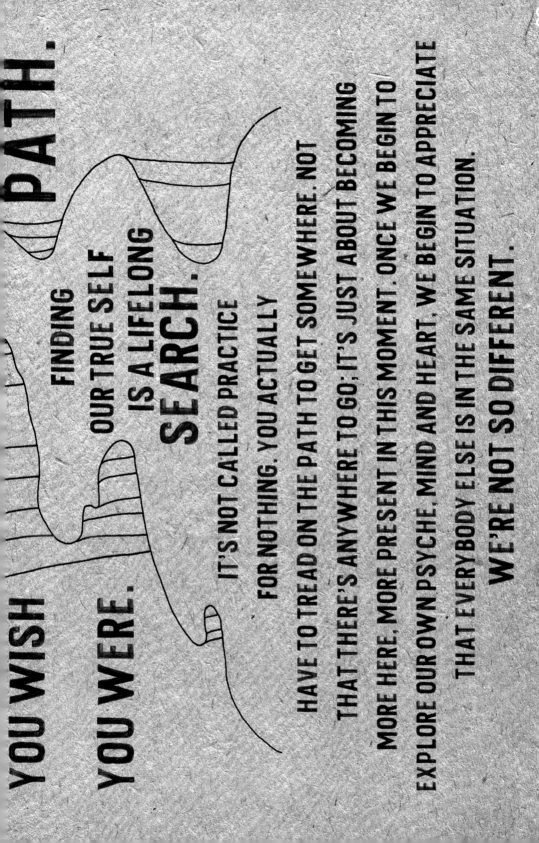

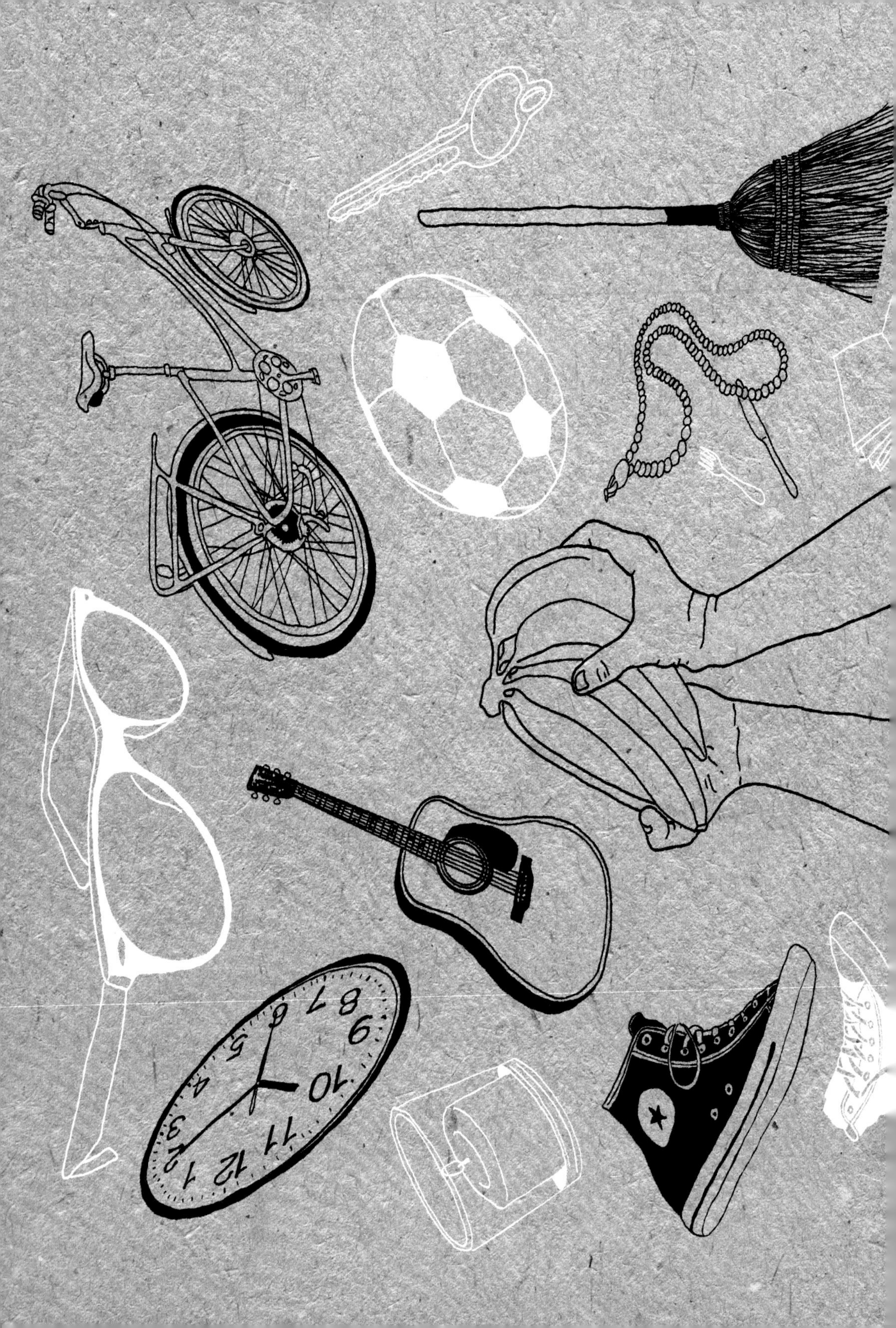

AS YOU BEGIN TO OPEN AND EXPLORE THIS JOURNEY, YOU CAN TAKE THE STUFF

OF YOUR DAILY LIFE AND START TO OFFER IT UP. WHAT YOU DO IS YOU BEGIN TO

CONSECRATE YOUR LIFE. INSTEAD OF GOD **BEING** SOME KIND OF ABSTRACTION THAT

YOU DEAL WITH ON SUNDAYS OR THAT WAS CONNECTED WITH YOUR PARENTS, OR

IS SOMETHING NICE, YOU BEGIN TO RECOGNIZE THIS AS YOUR TRUE IDENTITY, JUST

A LITTLE BIT, SO THAT WITH EVERYTHING YOU'RE **DOING**. YOU DON'T HAVE TO

CHANGE A STEP IN THE DANCE. YOU DON'T HAVE TO DROP OUT. YOU DON'T HAVE TO GO

TO A CAVE. YOU DON'T HAVE TO SHAVE YOUR HEAD OR WEAR FUNNY CLOTHES OR DO

ANYTHING. THE PROCESS CHANGES IN YOUR **BEING**, NOT IN YOUR **DOING**. AND

AS YOUR **BEING** CHANGES, YOUR **DOING** WILL CHANGE, BUT IT WILL CHANGE

VERY SUBTLY, SO THAT YOU MIGHT DRIVE THE SAME BUS YESTERDAY THAT YOU DRIVE

TOMORROW, BUT TOMORROW WHEN YOU DRIVE THE BUS, EVERYBODY THAT GETS

ON THE BUS GETS A CERTAIN VIBRATIONAL SPACE CREATED BY YOUR **BEING** THAT

ALLOWS THEM TO NOTICE A PLACE IN THEM THAT'S JUST A LITTLE DEEPER.

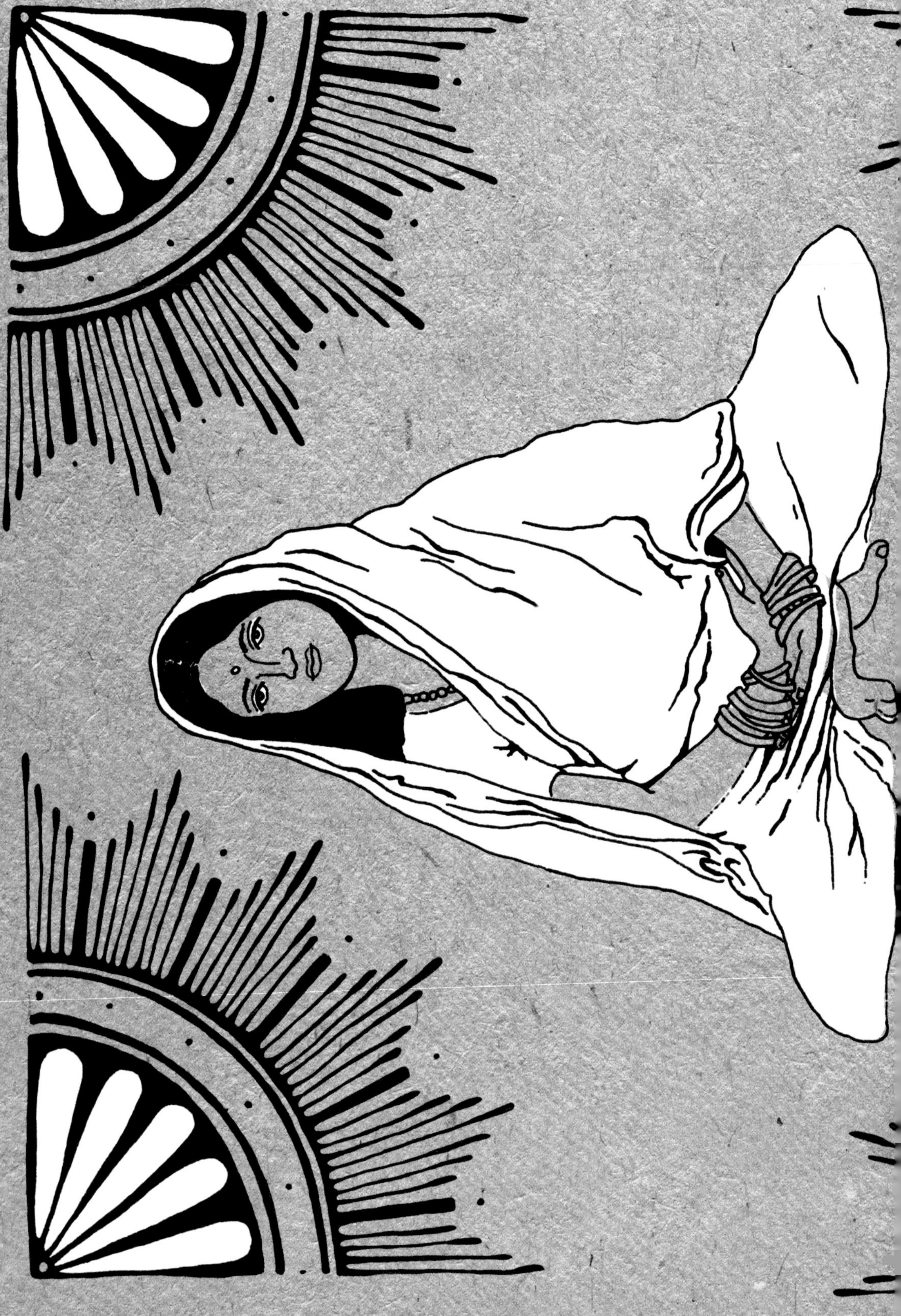

ANANDAMAYI MA

ALL THAT YOU DO TO MAINTAIN YOUR LIFE, YOUR EVERYDAY WORK AND PLAY, ALL YOUR ATTEMPTS TO EARN A LIVING, SHOULD BE DONE WITH SINCERITY, LOVE, AND DEVOTION, WITH A FIRM CONVICTION THAT TRUE LIVING MEANS VIRTUALLY PERFECTING ONE'S SPIRITUAL EXISTENCE IN TUNE WITH THE UNIVERSE.

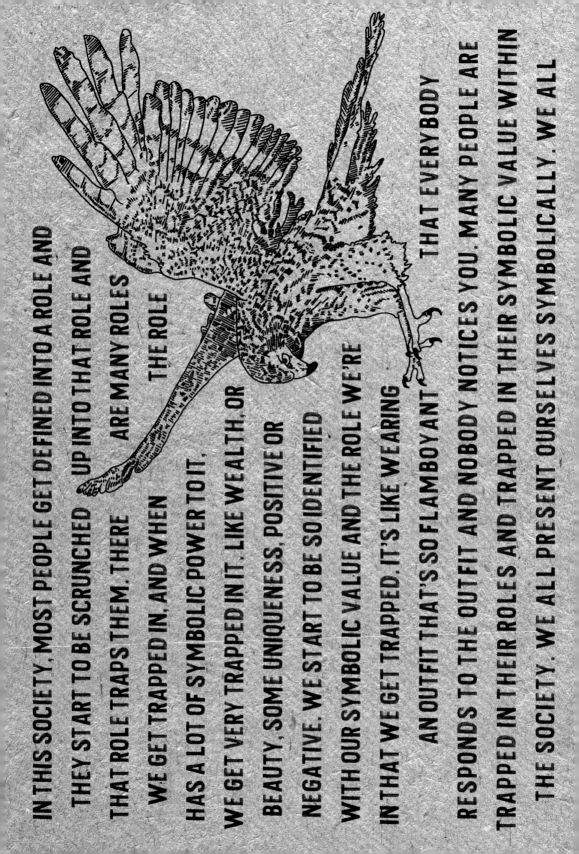

IN THIS SOCIETY, MOST PEOPLE GET DEFINED INTO A ROLE AND THEY START TO BE SCRUNCHED UP INTO THAT ROLE AND THAT ROLE TRAPS THEM. THERE ARE MANY ROLES THE ROLE WE GET TRAPPED IN, AND WHEN HAS A LOT OF SYMBOLIC POWER TO IT, WE GET VERY TRAPPED IN IT. LIKE WEALTH, OR BEAUTY, SOME UNIQUENESS, POSITIVE OR NEGATIVE. WE START TO BE SO IDENTIFIED WITH OUR SYMBOLIC VALUE AND THE ROLE WE'RE IN THAT WE GET TRAPPED. IT'S LIKE WEARING AN OUTFIT THAT'S SO FLAMBOYANT THAT EVERYBODY RESPONDS TO THE OUTFIT AND NOBODY NOTICES YOU. MANY PEOPLE ARE TRAPPED IN THEIR ROLES AND TRAPPED IN THEIR SYMBOLIC VALUE WITHIN THE SOCIETY. WE ALL PRESENT OURSELVES SYMBOLICALLY. WE ALL

PROJECT WHO WE THINK WE ARE IN THE CLOTHES WE WEAR, IN THE WAY WE WALK, IN THE WAY WE LOOK AT OTHER PEOPLE. THAT'S ONLY THE IMAGE WE HAVE OF OURSELVES PROJECTED OUTWARD. SOMETIMES THAT'S VERY VERY STRONG. YOU'RE SO BUSY BEING *SOMEBODY* THAT EVERYONE REACTS TO YOUR *SOMEBODY-NESS*, AND NOBODY REACTS TO YOUR *NOBODY-NESS*. NOBODY REACTS TO THE PART OF YOU THAT'S THE *I*, NOT TO *ME*. AND SO IT'S INTERESTING TO LEARN IN THIS LIFETIME HOW TO INHABIT ROLES LIGHTLY, HOW TO INHABIT THEM WITH LOVE AND WITH JOY AND WITH PASSION, AND WITH EMPTINESS. HOW TO DELIGHT IN THE GAME, IN THE DANCE, IN THE LILA, IN THE PLAY, AND BEGIN TO SEE YOUR LIFE EXPERIENCES AS GRACE, AS A SET OF OPPORTUNITIES THROUGH WHICH YOU CAN BECOME FREE.

TO BE FREE MEANS TO OPEN YOUR HEART AND YOUR BEING TO THE FULLNESS OF WHO YOU ARE, BECAUSE WHEN YOU ARE RESTING IN THE PLACE OF UNITY YOU CAN TRULY HONOR AND APPRECIATE OTHERS AND THE INCREDIBLE DIVERSITY OF THE UNIVERSE. IF YOU GET TOO FOCUSED ON INDIVIDUAL DIFFERENCES, YOU LOSE IT. BECAUSE BEHIND ALL THE DIFFERENT FACES IS THE ONE. IF YOU ONLY SEE THE ONE AND DON'T SEE ALL THE

DIFFERENT FACES, YOU LOSE IT. IF YOU ONLY SEE THE UNITY AND DON'T SEE THE UNIQUENESS, YOU MISS THE MARK. WHAT A CHALLENGE FOR US, TO KEEP THE BALANCE, AND TO SEE OUR LIVES AS INSTRUMENTS FOR BRINGING THAT BALANCE BACK INTO THE SOCIAL FABRIC. THE MINUTE YOU GET LOST IN IDENTIFICATION WITH YOUR PERSONALITY TO THE EXCLUSION OF IDENTIFICATION WITH YOUR SOUL, YOU LOSE IT. RIGHT? THAT'S WHAT HAPPENS. AND THEN A THOUSAND TIMES EACH DAY YOU LOSE IT, AND IF YOU GET CAUGHT IN YOUR SOUL TO THE EXCLUSION OF YOUR PERSONALITY YOU LOSE IT EQUALLY AS MUCH AND THAT'S THE BALANCE OF US AS HUMAN BEINGS.

I THINK IT'S IMPORTANT TO HAVE JUST AN APPRECIATION FOR THE

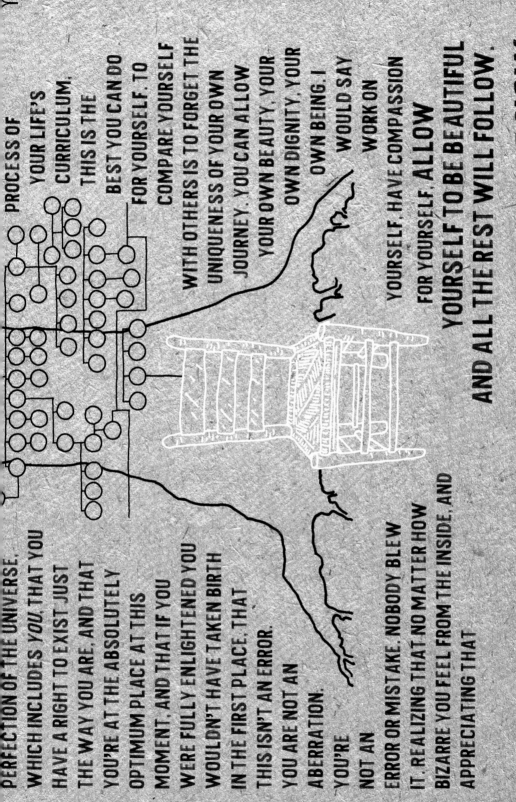

PERFECTION OF THE UNIVERSE, WHICH INCLUDES *YOU*, THAT YOU HAVE A RIGHT TO EXIST JUST THE WAY YOU ARE, AND THAT YOU'RE AT THE ABSOLUTELY OPTIMUM PLACE AT THIS MOMENT, AND THAT IF YOU WERE FULLY ENLIGHTENED YOU WOULDN'T HAVE TAKEN BIRTH IN THE FIRST PLACE, THAT THIS ISN'T AN ERROR. YOU ARE NOT AN ABERRATION. YOU'RE NOT AN ERROR OR MISTAKE. NOBODY BLEW IT, REALIZING THAT NO MATTER HOW BIZARRE YOU FEEL FROM THE INSIDE, AND APPRECIATING THAT

PROCESS OF YOUR LIFE'S CURRICULUM. THIS IS THE BEST YOU CAN DO FOR YOURSELF. TO COMPARE YOURSELF WITH OTHERS IS TO FORGET THE UNIQUENESS OF YOUR OWN JOURNEY. YOU CAN ALLOW YOUR OWN BEAUTY, YOUR OWN DIGNITY, YOUR OWN BEING. I WOULD SAY WORK ON YOURSELF. HAVE COMPASSION FOR YOURSELF. *ALLOW YOURSELF TO BE BEAUTIFUL* AND ALL THE REST WILL FOLLOW.

BE AT HOME IN THE UNIVERSE. *BE HERE NOW.*

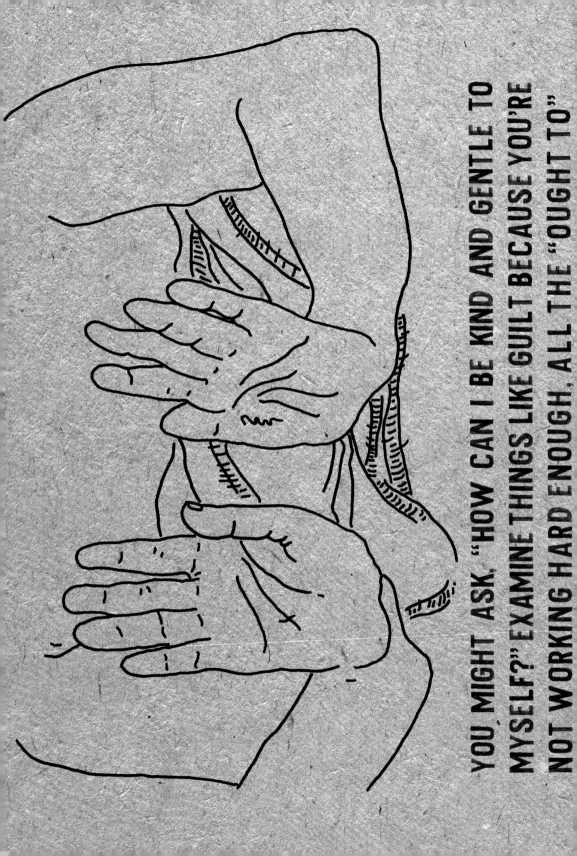

YOU MIGHT ASK, "HOW CAN I BE KIND AND GENTLE TO MYSELF?" EXAMINE THINGS LIKE GUILT BECAUSE YOU'RE NOT WORKING HARD ENOUGH, ALL THE "OUGHT TO"

AND "SHOULDS" YOU RUTHLESSLY DRIVE YOURSELF ON WITH, ALL THE FEELINGS OF NOT BEING GOOD ENOUGH, OR THAT YOU OUGHT TO BE MORE SPIRITUAL OR CONSCIOUS OR SOMETHING MORE THAN YOU ARE. EXAMINE THESE.

YOU HAVE TO LOVE YOURSELF. THE FOUNDATION OF ALL OF THIS WORK IS LOVING YOURSELF. LOVING YOURSELF AS A SOUL. THE JUDGING MIND IN YOUR HEAD THAT SAYS, "I'M NO GOOD. I'VE DONE EVIL THINGS." THAT'S ALL IN YOUR MIND. BUT WHEN YOU STEP BACK FROM THAT AND GO TO THE HEART, TO THE SOUL, YOU FIND LOVE BECAUSE THE SOUL LOVES ITSELF, AND THE SOUL IS WHAT YOU REALLY ARE, NOT YOUR EGO.

YOUR EGO IS A DREAM. [113]

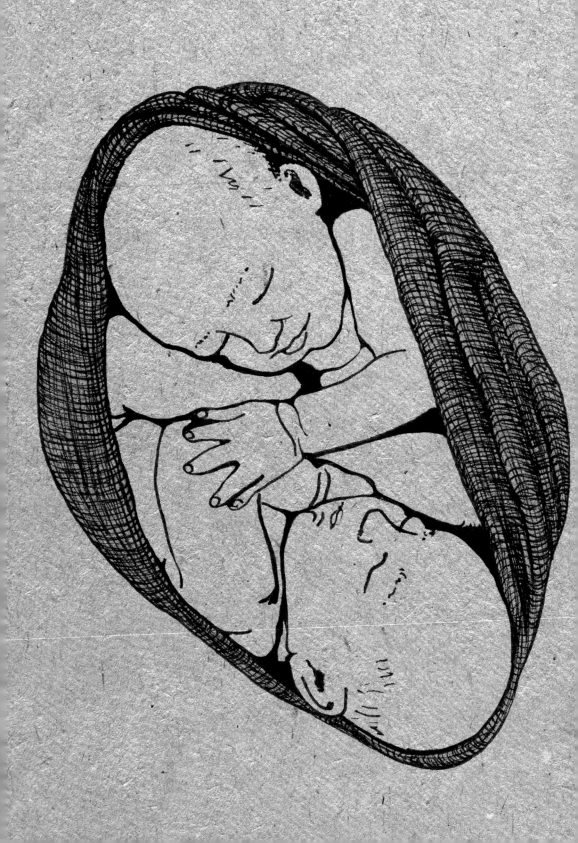

WE'RE HERE TO AWAKEN FROM THE ILLUSION OF SEPERATENESS.

AS WE GROW IN CONSCIOUSNESS, THERE WILL BE MORE COMPASSION AND MORE LOVE, AND THEN THE BARRIERS BETWEEN PEOPLE, BETWEEN RELIGIONS, BETWEEN NATIONS WILL BEGIN TO FALL.

WE ARE PART OF THE UNIVERSE, LIKE A TREE IS, OR LIKE GRASS IS, OR LIKE WATER IS, LIKE STORMS, LIKE ROSES. WE ARE JUST PART OF IT ALL. WHEN YOU SMELL A FLOWER, YOU ARE THE FLOWER. YOU ARE ONE.

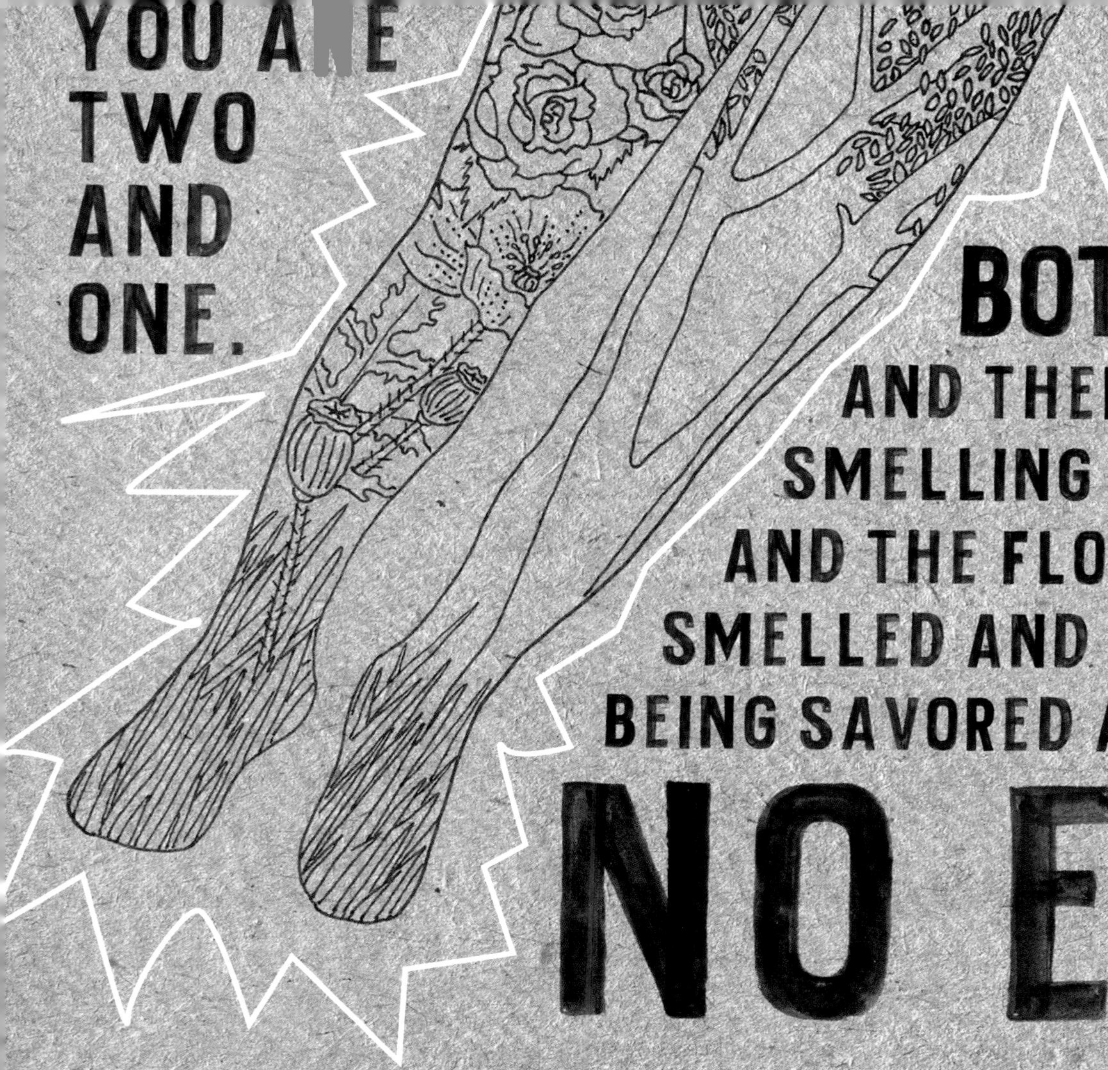

YOU ARE
TWO
AND
ONE.

BOTH AT ONCE.

AND THERE IS NOBODY
SMELLING THE FLOWER.
AND THE FLOWER IS BEING
SMELLED AND THE SMELL IS
BEING SAVORED AND YET THERE IS

NO EGO.

WHO YOU ARE IS BEYOND TIME, BEYOND SPACE, WITHOUT FORM, WITHOU

E, ABSOLUTE KNOWLEDGE, ABSOLUTE WISDOM. IN TRUTH THERE IS NOWHERE WHERE YOU AR

U ARE, AND YOU ALWAYS WILL BE. YOU ARE THE ANCIENT ONE. THERE IS NO

CARNATION, A LEARNING HOW TO LIVE ON EVERY PLANE S

REST

IMIT. YOU ARE IN EVERYTHING. EVERYTHING IS IN YOU. YOU ARE THE BLISS OF THE UNIVERSE. YOU ARE ABSOLUTE EXIST

ND THERE IS NOWHERE WHERE YOU ARE NOT. WHO YOU ARE IS INVULNERABLE. YOU ALWAYS WER

E FOR WHO YOU ARE. THROUGH A QUIET MIND, AN OPEN HEART, AN HONORING O

LTANEOUSLY, IMPECCABLY. BECOME. KNOW YOUR ORIGINAL

IN LOVE.

OUT OF AN INFINITE VARIETY OF PLANES

THREE PLANES OF AWARENESS OR

THREE SPHERES OF AWARENESS

DON'T THINK THAT PLANES, OR
SPHERES, MEAN HIGHER OR BETTER.
THEY'RE JUST DIFFERENT FROM ONE
ANOTHER.

I am the void, who manifests as the
one, who becomes the many, who
has a unique set of factors to
work out, through a unique
astral, psychological,
& physical body.

That's what I'm doing on earth.
I have taken a body
to do certain work &
when I finish that
work, I will
drop that
body.

AWARENESS

IF YOU GO IN & IN & IN & IN YOU
WILL COME TO THE AWARE-
NESS • INCLUDES SOUL &
EGO • IS CONSCIOUS-
NESS • IS THE ONE • IS
LOVE • IS TRUTH • IS
ONENESS • IS THE
MYSTICAL PART OF
US • IS THE SAME IN
YOU & ME • A UNIVER-
SAL SHARED HIGHER
AWARENESS • IS THE

SOUL

IS ANOTHER LEVEL
OF WHO YOU ARE • A
DIFFERENT PLANE OF
CONSCIOUSNESS •
DOESN'T DIE • IS THE
WITNESS WITNESS-
ING THAT THOUGHT •
WITNESSING THE
INCARNATION •
WITNESSING THE
SUFFERING • WIT-
NESSING KARMA

THIS IS THE EFFECT • IS FORMLESS • IS CREATION PRESERVATION & DE-STRUCTION • THE NO-NAME & THE THOUSAND NAMES • IT'S ALL THE FACETS THAT KEEP POINTING YOU TOWARDS THAT WHICH IS BEYOND FACET, OR, EMBRACES ALL FACETS • GOD, GURU & AND SELF AS ONE • OUR TRUE NATURE • IS PURE LOVE • IS WISDOM • IS PEACE • IS COM-PASSION • IS JOY • DESCRIBED AS THE VOID • IT'S UNSPEAKABLE. UNKNOWABLE. UNSEEABLE. INCONCEIVABLE • EXISTS BEFORE THE WORD. BEFORE THE VIBRATORY UNIQUENESS • IS GOING NOWHERE & IS COMING FROM NOWHERE • INSIDE & OUT SIDE OF EVERYTHING • THE ONE AWARENESS IN MULTIPLICITY OF FORMS • CREATES SOUL • IS THE STILL SMALL VOICE OF GOD WITHIN • "I AM" CONSCIOUSNESS • WISDOM COMES FROM THIS PLANE OF CONSCIOUSNESS • OMNIPRESENT • OCEAN OF LOVE • IS THE UNIVERSE •

BEING WORLD OUT • LOVES EVERY-THING • IS INFINITE. NO TIME, NO SPACE • LIV-ING WITH LOVE • IS PURE • COMES FROM THE ONE • LOVES & IS LOVE • THE MIDDLE GROUND. THE MIDDLE LEVEL • REINCARNATES • IS SOME) PLACE YOU CAN GO FROM WHICH YOU CAN SEE YOUR EGO • IS WORKING OUT IT'S OWN UNIQUE KARMA. PSYCHIC DNA. UNDIGESTED ATTACHMENTS, AVERSIONS & ATTRACTIONS • GOES THROUGH VAST CYCLES OF TIME • IS CALLED MINDFULNESS • HAS COMPASSION • SEES EVERYONE AS A SOUL • IS A SPIRITUAL BODY • IS A SPIRITUAL IDENTITY • DOES NOT FREAK WHEN YOU DIE, BECAUSE IT FUNCTIONS IN LOVE • MEETS TOGETHER WITH OTH-ER SOULS TO ENJOY & APPRECIATE & FEEL CONCERN FOR ALL • COMMUNICATES WITH ONE ANOTHER ON THE FIELD OF LOVE • HAS ONLY 1 MOTIVE: MERGING WITH THE BELOVED. MERGING WITH THE ONE • DOESN'T HAVE NEED FOR MEMORY • LEARNS SOMETHING WITH EACH INCARNATION • COMES OUT OF AWARENESS • IS NOT THE BODY • IS INNOCENT • BRINGS OUT THE BEAUTY IN EACH OF US • CLOSER TO THE ONE. THE SOURCE • YOU CAN FEEL IT IN YOUR HEART • IDENTICAL & INTERCONNECTED TO OTHER SOULS • IDENTIFICA-TION WITH SOUL CREATES SPACIOUSNESS, CALM, & TRANSFORMATION • HAS NO GENDER OR SEXUAL IDENTITY • IS THE ESSENCE • CREATES EGO • THE WITNESS TO THE STORY • IS HERE TO LEARN SOMETHING ABOUT SUFFERING & LOVE •

EGO

IS BORN & DIES • IS WHO YOU THINK YOU ARE • THE PHYSICAL BODY, PERSONALITY & PSYCHOLOGY • IS AFRAID OF DEATH • IS GOOD & EVIL • FEELS PAIN • ACTS & DOES • GROWS OLD. HAS SEX. DESIRES. FEARS. DEPRESSIONS. ELATIONS. ANXIETIES. LONELINESS. HOPES. GREED. LUST & JEALOUSY • HAS JUDGMENTS & AVERSIONS • CAN COMMUNICATE WITH THE SOUL THROUGH THE IMAGINATION. THE MIND & FEELINGS • INHABITS & GETS CAUGHT IN ROLES • IS "SOMEBODY" THAT GOES THROUGH "SOMEBODY" TRAINING • IDENTIFIES WITH THE "I" & INDIVIDUALITY. THE MIND & THOUGHTS • SUFFERS • IS SOCIALIZED TO DEFINE WHO YOU THINK YOU ARE & WHAT THE GAME IS ABOUT • COMES WITH YOUR INCARNATION • HAS MANY MOTIVES • IS SURRENDERED IN DEATH • INCLUDES THE PHYSICAL, MENTAL, EMOTIONAL BODIES • WORRIES • LOOKS TO OTHERS FOR APPROVAL • CAN ACCESS LOVING AWARENESS • IS LOVE • BELIEVES MATERIAL REALITY TO BE REAL • HAS UNIQUE ASTROLOGY & ASTRAL IDENTITY • THINKS IT'S A SEPARATE ENTITY FROM GOD • HAS ATTACHMENTS • IS A SOUL MANIFESTING TO WORK OUT IT'S UNIQUE KARMA • IS GOD IN DRAG. OR GOD IN FORM • IS THE ACTOR IN THE STORY/INCARNATION • CAN BECOME FREE • IS A VEHICLE FOR LIBERATION • DEVELOPS MODELS & BELIEFS • IS BUSY BEING "SOMEBODY" • MAKES ITSELF SAFE IN AN UNRULY WORLD • FILTERS OUT IRRELEVANT INFO • HAS GENDER & SEXUALITY •

YOU SIT AND YOU ASK, "WHO AM I?".

AND YOU SAY, "I AM NOT MY SENSES."

YOU CAN BE AWARE OF YOUR 👁 SEEING, YOUR

HEARING, YOUR 🖐 FEELING, AND YOUR MIND PRODUCING THOUGHTS.

THOUGHT AFTER THOUGHT AFTER

THOUGHT AFTER THOUGHTS ARE SEDUCTIVE, BUT YOU DON'T HAVE TO IDENTIFY

WITH THEM. HAVE YOU EVER NOTICED YOUR 👂 HEARING? YOU

GO INSIDE UNTIL YOU CAN. SO TO SPEAK, WATCH YOUR 👂 HEARING.

YOU CAN SIT BACK AND WATCH THE WHOLE PROCESS UNFOLD. YOU

WATCH YOUR 👄 SMELL AND YOUR 👄 TASTE AND YOUR SKIN 🖐.

AND THEN YOU CONTINUE ON AND YOU SAY, "I AM NOT

MY ORGANS OF MOTION." YOUR [legs], YOUR [arm].

AND THEN YOU GO THROUGH YOUR INTERNAL ORGANS.

YOUR [heart] BEATING, YOUR [lungs] BREATHING, YOUR STOMACH

AND [intestines] DIGESTING, AND SO ON. AND THEN YOU'RE LEFT

WITH ONE THING, WHICH ARE YOUR [THOUGHTS]. AND THE FINAL

STATEMENT IS: I AM NOT THIS [THOUGHT]. YOU IDENTIFY

NOT WITH THE [THOUGHTS], BUT WITH THE AWARENESS OF THE [AWARENESS]

LOVING AWARENESS. TO BRING TO EVERYTHING YOU TURN YOUR

[THOUGHTS]. TO IS TO BE [LOVE]. THIS MOMENT IS [LOVE].

THE PART OF MY MIND THAT IS IN THE UN... AND EMOTIONAL DATA.

MIND TO ...

...TIFYING WITH THE WITNESS HAS BECOME MY METHOD FOR CULTIVATING

THOUGHTS, IDENTIFIES WITH EGO, IDENTIFIES WITH SENSORY

THE MIND IDENTIFIES WITH...

...ND AND HEART. THE EGO AND THE SOUL. IDEN...

ROLE TO

YOUR INCARNATION IS RULED

SOUL WITNESSES THE MIND, WITNESSES THE INCARNATION, WITNESSES THE UNIVERSE, WITH A NEUTRAL AWARENES

SE, BUT NOT TRAPPED BY IT.

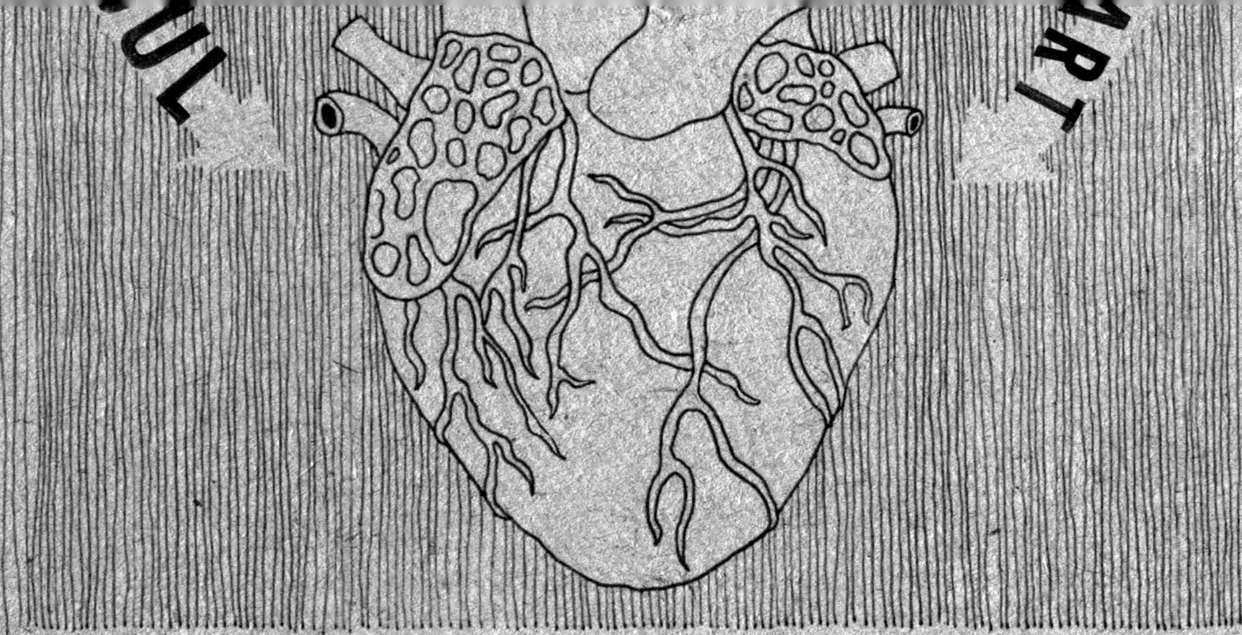

THIS LIFE IS ABOUT FINDING A WAY TO BE IN THE WORLD THAT CONNECTS YOU TO YOUR SOUL. THAT IS WHERE THE SPIRITUAL DIMENSION BEGINS, AND THAT'S A PART THAT LOOKS AT THE UNIVERSE AND JUST SEES IT AS IT IS. **LIVING FROM THE SOUL IS VERY MUCH A HEART-CENTERED JOURNEY.**

OUR JOURNEY IS ABOUT BEING MORE DEEPLY INVOLVED IN LIFE AND YET LESS ATTACHED TO IT. I'M TALKING ABOUT WHAT IT MEANS TO BE IN THE WORLD BUT NOT OF THE WORLD, WHICH MEANS TO STAY OPEN TO THE HUMAN CONDITION, TO YOUR FEAR, LONGING, HOPES, JOYS, AROUSALS, DEPRESSION, LONELINESS, SELF-PITY, ANGER, JEALOUSY, AND AT THE SAME MOMENT, SIMULTANEOUSLY DEVELOP A S P A C I O U S N E S S THAT SURROUNDS IT. JUST LIKE SKY SURROUNDS CLOUDS. AND WHAT YOU DO AT FIRST, TO DEVELOP AN APPRECIATION OF THAT PART OF YOU THAT ISN'T FORM, THAT ISN'T WANTING, YEARNING, SEPARATE, NEEDFUL, YOU DO YOUR METHODS. YOU DO MEDITATION. YOU DO DEVOTION. YOU DO WHATEVER YOU DO. YOU STUDY. YOU GATHER WITH SATSANG. YOU DO THESE KINDS OF THINGS.

AND THEN, AS YOUR FAITH IN THAT PART OF YOU GETS STRONGER, YOU DON'T PUSH AWAY YOUR HUMAN EXPERIENCES AS MUCH. DON'T THINK YOU CAN AVOID LIFE AND GET FREE FROM IT AT THE SAME TIME. LIFE IS A SERIES OF EXPERIENCES. ALLOW THE RISK OF ATTACHMENT, AND ALSO BE CONSTANTLY CONNECTING TO THIS PART THAT HAS NOTHING TO DO WITH THE ATTACHMENT. IT DOESN'T MEAN YOU'RE NOT EXPERIENCING YOUR FEELINGS AND ALL THAT IS HAPPENING, BUT IT MEANS, IN ADDITION TO EXPERIENCING THEM, YOU'RE ALSO CULTIVATING

SPACIOUSNESS.

YES, WE ARE COMPASSIONATE, BUT DON'T BE BUSY BEING COMPASSIONATE

YES IT IS ALL A DREAM AND WE ARE EMPTY,

BUT DON'T BE BUSY
BEING EMPTY.

I WATCH MY MIND KEEP SLOWING DOWN, AND SLOWING DOWN AND SLOWING DOWN, SLOWING DOWN, SLOWING DOWN UNTIL PRETTY SOON I SEE EACH THOUGHT ARISE, EXIST, AND PASS AWAY. THEN I SEE THE NEXT THOUGHT

ARISE, EXIST, PASS AWAY. AND THEN I SEE A SPACE BETWEEN EACH THOUGHT. IT GETS BIGGER AND BIGGER AS MY MIND SETTLES MORE DEEPLY AND THEN I GO INTO THE SPACE BETWEEN TWO THOUGHTS, AND THERE'S A BREAK IN CONSCIOUSNESS. AND THEN THE NEXT MOMENT I THINK, "I CAN BE ANYTHING I WANT." AND THEN I START TO

RECREATE THE UNIVERSE AFTER THAT.

WORKING ON OUR OWN CONSCIOUSNESS IS THE MOST IMPORTANT THING THAT WE ARE DOING AT ANY MOMENT, AND BEING LOVE IS A SUPREME CREATIVE ACT.

YOU ARE BOTH...

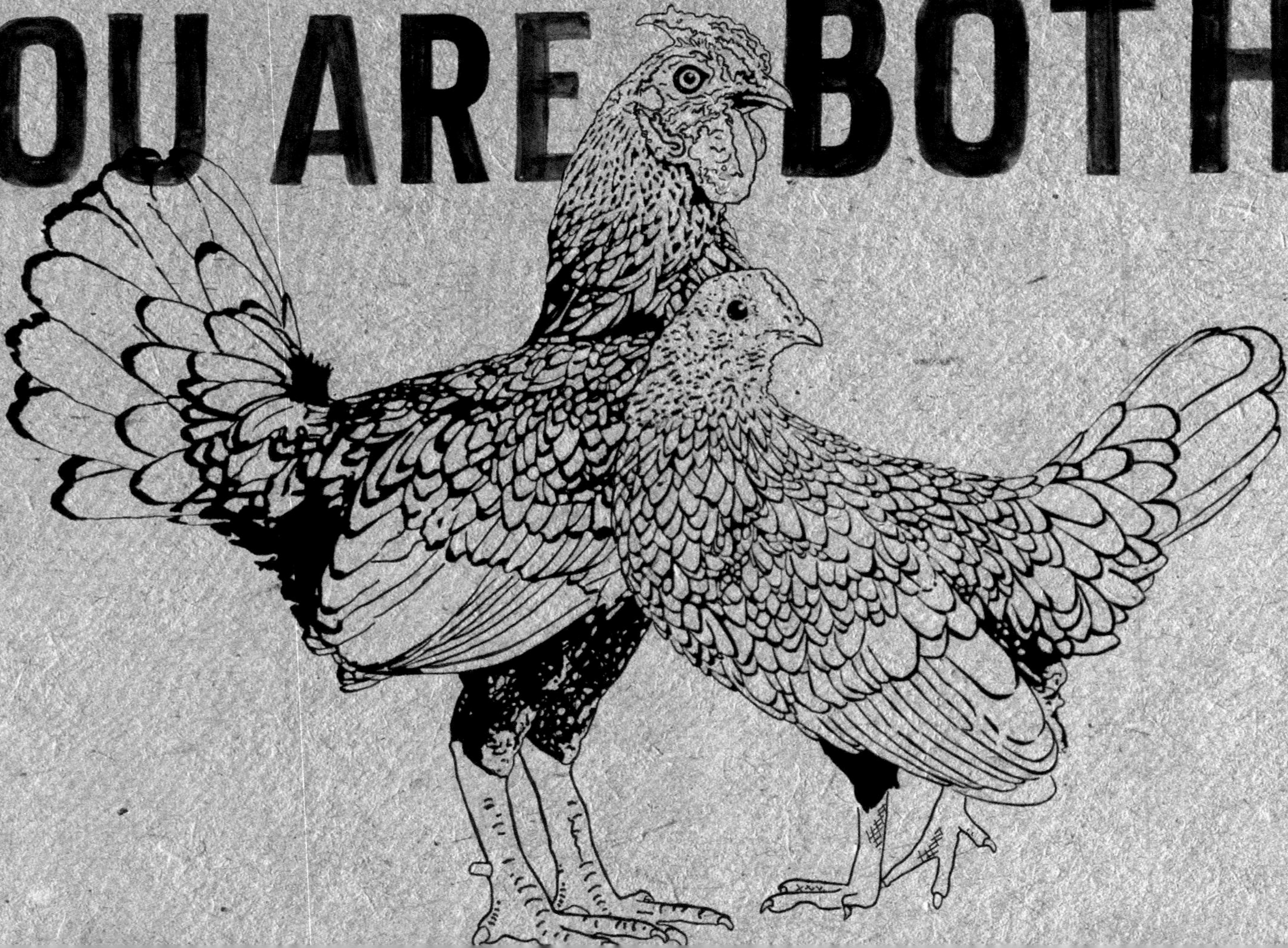

THE CREATOR AND THE CREATED.

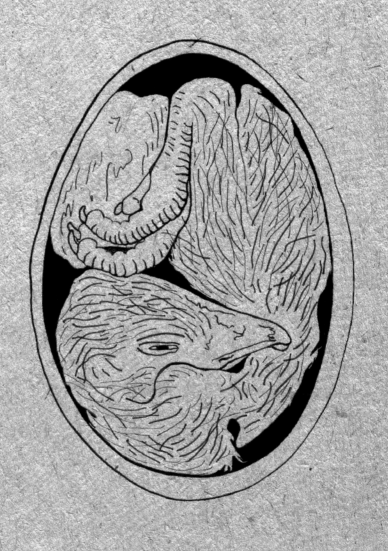

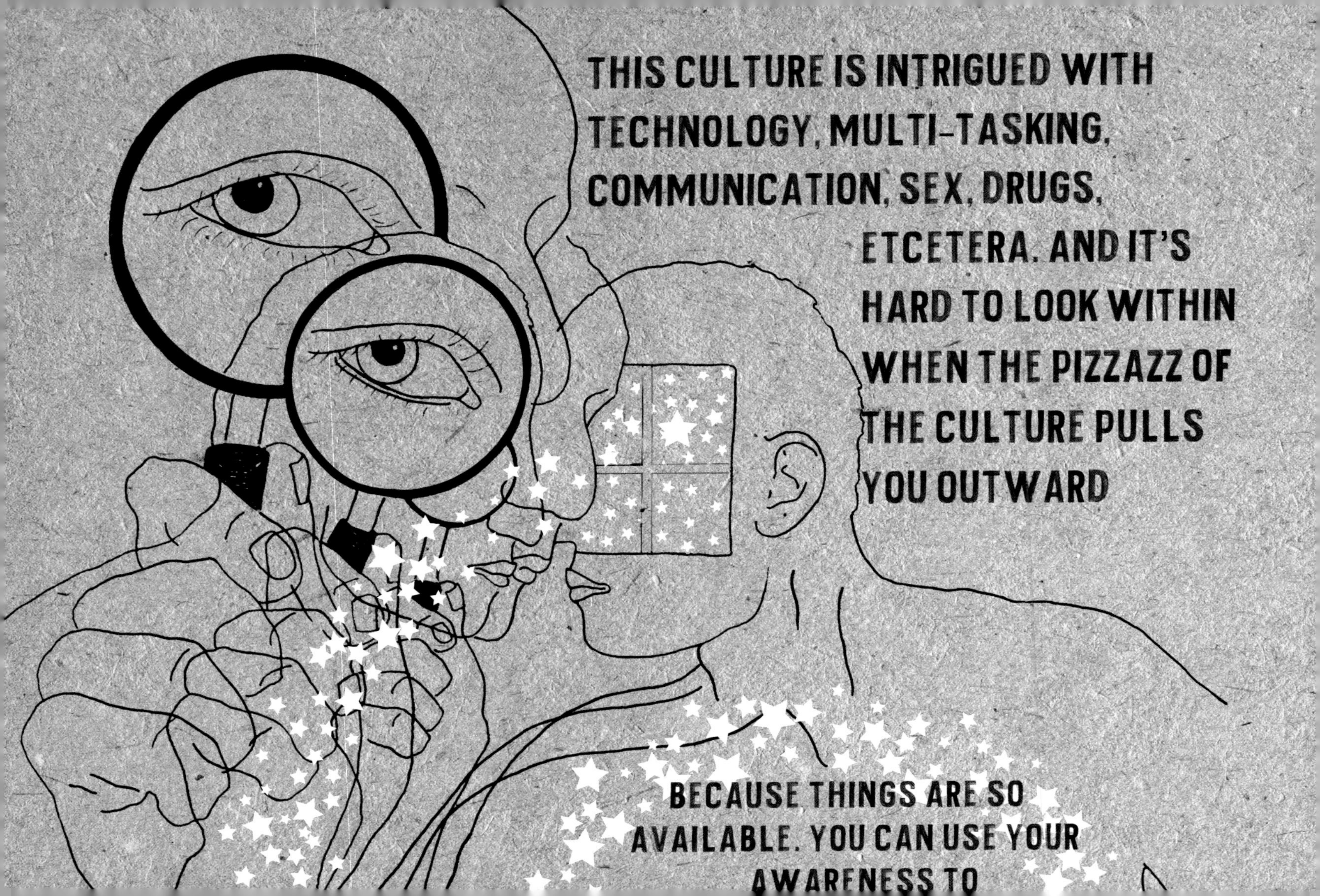

THIS CULTURE IS INTRIGUED WITH TECHNOLOGY, MULTI-TASKING, COMMUNICATION, SEX, DRUGS, ETCETERA. AND IT'S HARD TO LOOK WITHIN WHEN THE PIZZAZZ OF THE CULTURE PULLS YOU OUTWARD

BECAUSE THINGS ARE SO AVAILABLE. YOU CAN USE YOUR AWARENESS TO

GO INWARD. TO FIND YOUR INNER GURU, YOUR TRUE SPIRITUAL SELF, YOU HAVE TO LOOK WITHIN.

ONE OF THE DOORWAYS TO THAT HIGHER SELF IS THROUGH THE CULTIVATION OF YOUR INTUITIVE WISDOM. THE INTUITION, THE IMPECCABLE, INTUITIVE ACTION, HAS TO COME FROM A BLENDING OF HUMANITY AND DIVINITY. AS YOU LEARN TO LISTEN TO AND TRUST YOUR INTUITION, YOU WILL FIND A QUIET PLACE IN THE HEART OF YOUR BEING THAT IS WISE AND CAN GUIDE YOUR ACTIONS. INTUITIVELY, WE ARE WISE BECAUSE WE SEE THE WHOLE INCARNATION. THAT'S WISDOM THAT YOU CAN UNDERSTAND BY INTUITION. TRUST YOUR INTUITION. LISTEN TO YOUR HEART. ALWAYS TRUST YOUR INNER VOICE.

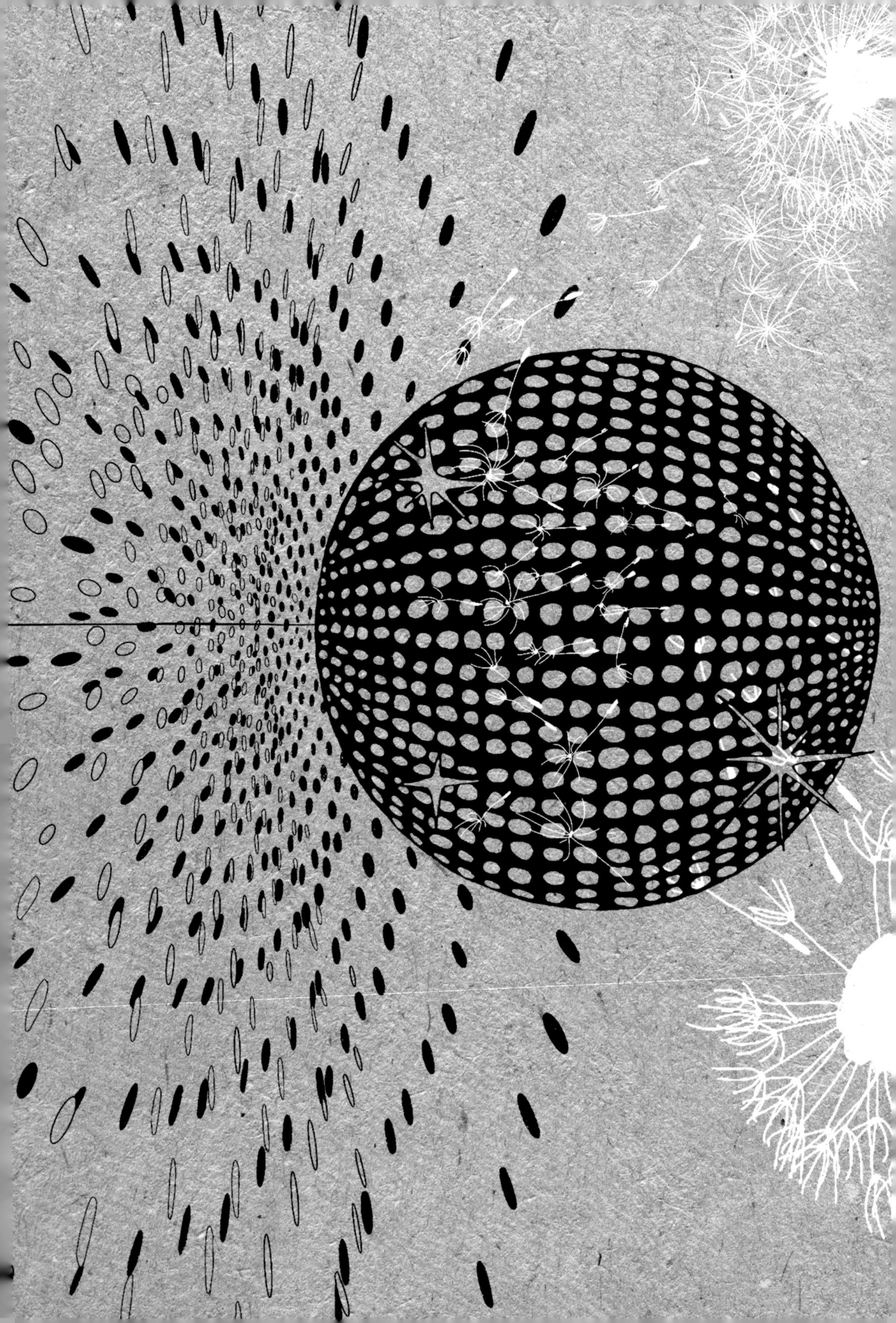

YOU MAKE A DECISION BASED ON THE OPTIMUM INFORMATION YOU HAVE AVAILABLE NOW AND BY QUIETING YOUR MIND, AND BY DEEPLY FEELING THE PRESENT. IF YOU ARE QUIET ENOUGH, AND CAN FIND THE PLACE IN YOU THAT IS BEHIND TIME, THEN YOUR CHOICES CONTAIN WITHIN THEM THE NATURE OF THE WAY THINGS WILL CHANGE. WHEN YOU DON'T HAVE THAT MUCH CLARITY OF MIND, YOU MAKE A DECISION NOW, KNOWING FULL WELL THAT CONDITIONS MAY CHANGE TO MAKE IT INAPPROPRIATE LATER ON. IN A CHANGING ENVIRONMENT YOU HAVE TO UNDERSTAND THAT CONDITIONS WILL CHANGE. THE MINUTE YOU START TO TRY TO LIVE YOUR LIFE AS IF NOTHING WILL CHANGE, YOU BECOME AN ENEMY OF THE WAY OF THINGS. SO INSTEAD YOU LEARN TO DANCE WITH CHANGE. YOU LEARN TO LIVE MORE COMFORTABLY WITH LESS CERTAINTY ABOUT WHAT THE FUTURE HOLDS, OF WHO YOU'LL BE WHEN YOU GROW UP, OR HOW IT WILL ALL COME OUT.

SEEING THE POSSIBILITY IS INDEED DIFFERENT FROM BEING THE POSSIBILITY.

आदित्यहृदयस्तोत्र

ADITYA HRIDAYAM PUNYAM
SARV SHATRU VINASHANAM.

WHEN THE SUN
IS KEPT IN THE HEART,
ALL EVILS VANISH FROM LIFE.

FROM THE RAMAYANA

TRANSLATED BY K. K. SAH

I HAD AN INTERESTING TIME WITH THAT, BECAUSE IN BUDDHISM ONE OF THE THINGS IS "MAY ALL BEINGS BE HAPPY" AND IN THE METTA MEDITATION WE WERE DOING, IT'S "MAY WE BE ENABLED TO CARRY OUT OUR LIVES IN PEACE AND HAPPINESS." AND AS LONG AS I KEPT HAPPINESS AS THE POLAR OPPOSITE OF SADNESS, IT WAS LIKE KEEPING LOVE AS THE POLAR OPPOSITE OF HATE. AND THEN IT TURNS OUT THERE'S A SEMANTIC ISSUE OF WHICH LEVEL ARE YOU USING THE WORD AT, AND TO THE EXTENT THAT HAPPINESS MEANS "BEING IN HARMONY WITH WHAT IS," MEANING "BEING PEACEFULLY IN RELATIONSHIP TO EVERYTHING THAT IS," I FINALLY REALIZED THAT MY HAPPINESS ISN'T BASED ON THE SITUATION BEING THIS WAY OR THAT WAY; MY HAPPINESS IS ONE THAT EMBRACES MY SADNESS. FINALLY, MY LOVE IS ONE THAT EMBRACES MY OWN HATE.

AND THAT QUALITY OF HAPPINESS FROM JUST BEING IN RELATIONSHIP TO THE UNIVERSE AS IT IS, NOT BECAUSE IT'S THIS WAY OR BECAUSE IT'S THAT WAY, IS THIS DEEPER QUALITY OF HAPPINESS THAT IS WHAT THIS BUDDHIST PRAYER IS ASKING FOR.

SO I THINK WE'RE PLAYING WITH THE POLARITY OF HAPPINESS AND SADNESS. NOW YOU UNDERSTAND, FINALLY, THAT THE WAY YOU LOOK AT YOUR SADNESS IS NOT AS SOMETHING TO PUSH AWAY. YES, THERE IS SADNESS IN LIFE, AND MY SADNESS ALSO CAME OUT OF MY TRUTH. SEE, WHEN YOU COME UP FOR AIR OUT OF A LOT OF SADNESS YOU WANT TO CLING TO YOUR HAPPINESS. BUT AS LONG AS YOU ARE CLINGING TO ANYTHING AND PUSHING ANYTHING AWAY YOU'RE VULNERABLE. IT'S GOT YOU; YOU'RE TRAPPED. YOU'RE ALWAYS FRIGHTENED, BECAUSE YOU'RE ALWAYS ANTICIPATING THE SLIP BACK INTO SADNESS. AND FINALLY YOU HAVE TO EMBRACE IT INTO YOURSELF. ALL OF IT. SO I'D SAY NOW THAT YOU HAVE LEARNED TO BE HAPPY, YOU CAN TURN AROUND AND LOOK BACK AT YOUR SADNESS AND START TO ALLOW THAT THAT'S A PART OF YOU TOO. UNTIL YOU'VE EMBRACED ALL OF IT INTO YOURSELF.

I TELL YOU THAT YOU REALLY HAVE TO EXPECT YOUR HEART TO OPEN AND CLOSE LIKE AN ACCORDION. AND WHEN IT CLOSES IT WILL OPEN. AND WHEN IT OPENS IT WILL PROBABLY CLOSE. BECAUSE BEHIND CLOSINGS AND OPENINGS, HERE WE ARE. AND SO INSTEAD OF DRAMATIZING YOUR CLOSED HEART OR YOUR OPEN HEART, JUST ALLOW IT TO BE PART OF THE PROCESS OF LIFE. AND BE PATIENT WITH YOURSELF, BECAUSE IT IS VERY CLEAR TO ME THAT THE SHADOW IS THE GREATEST TEACHER OF HOW TO COME TO THE LIGHT. I DON'T ASK FOR SUFFERING, BUT WHEN IT COMES ALONG IT CERTAINLY TURNS OUT TO BE GRACE, EVEN THOUGH I'M BEGRUDGING IT ALL THE TIME. YOU AND I LIVE IN A WORLD WHERE IT'S HARD TO KEEP YOUR HEART FULLY OPEN BECAUSE IT HURTS SO BAD, BECAUSE THERE IS SO MUCH SUFFERING. BUT I WILL TELL YOU. YOU CAN'T AFFORD TO CLOSE IT. AND SO WHEN IT BECOMES UNBEARABLE, YOU DO WHAT YOU DO WITH ANOTHER BEING BUT NEVER PUT THEM OUT OF YOUR HEART. YOU CAN SAY NO TO SOMEBODY, YOU CAN OPPOSE THEM, YOU CAN DO WHAT IS WITHIN YOUR ROLE AND DHARMA THAT YOU NEED TO DO. BUT IF IT INVOLVES CLOSING YOUR HEART, YOU CAN'T AFFORD IT. AND TO KEEP YOUR HEART FULLY OPEN WITH ANOTHER BEING REALLY IS SOUL BUSINESS. SO EVERY TIME I FORGET I'M DEALING WITH ANOTHER SOUL AND I GET CAUGHT IN THE DANCE OF ROLES THAT WE AS EGOS ARE

IN, I CAN FEEL IT IN MY HEART
AND IT HURTS SO BAD. YOU
SHOULD BE ABLE TO DO WHAT
YOU DO WITH ANOTHER
HUMAN BEING WITHOUT
FORGETTING THAT YOU
LOVE THIS SOUL AS
A SOUL: NOT THEIR
ACTIONS, BUT
THEIR ESSENCE,
THEIR BEING.

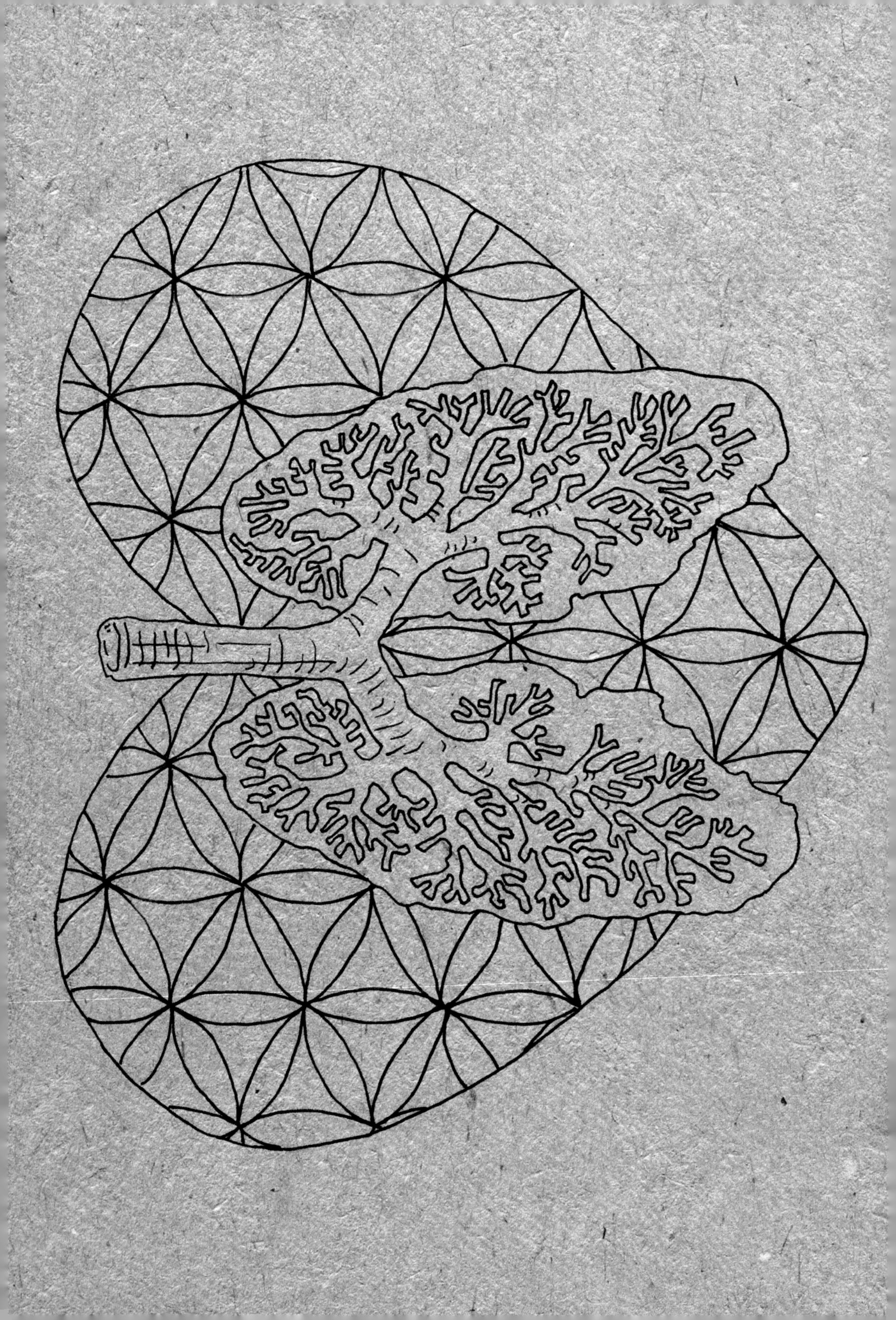

BREATHE DEEPLY, IN AND OUT OF THE HEART AS THOUGH IT HAD

NOSTRILS, RIGHT IN AND OUT OF THE HEART. YOU CAN USE THAT BREATH TO FERRET OUT

THOSE PLACES IN YOU WHERE THERE IS A DEEP SADNESS OR SOME DEEP ATTACHMENTS

THAT ARE SLOWING YOUR PROGRESS. LET THEM COME FORTH AND LET THEM GO GIVE

THEM UP. KEEP BREATHING THEM OUT, THE SADNESS DEEP WITHIN YOUR HEART THAT

HAS CLOSED YOU OFF. KEEP BRINGING THEM FORWARD. KEEP GOING IN AND IN UNTIL

YOU'RE ALL THE WAY BACK TO YOUR SPINE. KEEP ALLOWING THE BREATH TO MORE

DEEPLY FILL THIS AREA, AND THEN BREATHE IT ALL OUT AGAIN. WE OPEN OUR HEART

WITH BREATH OR THOUGHTS. WE ASK TO BE ALLOWED TO FEEL THE LOVE THAT IS

ALWAYS THERE FOR US. IF WE REALLY OPEN OURSELVES AND ASK THAT IN TRUTH, WE

CAN POSSIBLY FEEL A WARMTH STARTING TO TOUCH US THAT WILL PERMEATE US AND

START A PROCESS OF OUR OPENING. WHEN WE FEEL LOVE WHEN WE ARE WITH EACH

OTHER, THAT OPENS US TO THE PLACE IN OURSELVES THAT IS LOVE. THE WAY TO DO IT IS

TO BECOME LOVE OURSELVES, WITHOUT CLINGING TO EACH OTHER. IF WE FOLLOW OUR

HEART, THERE IS NOTHING TO FEAR. THROUGH AN OPEN HEART, ONE HEARS THE UNIVERSE.

THERE'S ANOTHER PLANE OF
CONSCIOUSNESS THAT IS RIGHT HERE,
ACTUALLY. AND YOU LOOK AROUND AND
SEE THAT EVERYBODY'S *MISHPUCHA*.
EVERYBODY'S THE FAMILY. EVERYBODY'S
A SIBLING. OR IF YOU GO OUT FAR
ENOUGH, THERE'S ONLY ONE OF US. AND
YOU REALLY SEE IT, YOU EXPERIENCE
THE ONENESS OF THINGS. AND IT'S
SO CONNECTED AND SO BEAUTIFUL. THIS IS WHAT SATSANG,
OR *SANGHA*, IS. THIS IS THE COMMUNITY OF BEINGS WHO ARE
ACKNOWLEDGING THAT DUAL INTENTION: YOU WORK ON YOURSELF
AS AN OFFERING TO OTHERS, AND YOU WORK WITH OTHERS AS A
WAY OF WORKING ON YOURSELF. THE CIRCLE IS COMPLETE. AND
EVERYTHING IS PART OF THAT CIRCLE. AND IDEALLY YOU ENJOY THE
PROCESS, BECAUSE IT MAY BE AN UNENDING ONE.

IN THE HINDU EPIC THE *RAMAYANA*, RAM'S
WIFE, SITA, IS STOLEN AWAY BY THE BAD GUY,
RAVANA, AND NOBODY CAN FIND HER. WHAT
SEEMS LIKE A MYTHICAL BATTLE IS ACTUALLY
VERY DIRECTLY SYMBOLIC. RAM IS SYMBOLIC
OF THE FORCES OF LOVE AND CONSCIOUSNESS.
SITA REPRESENTS THE SOUL AND MOTHER OF
THIS PLANET.

RAVANA WAS ALSO A GREAT YOGI AND VERY CONSCIOUS, BUT WENT TO THE DARK SIDE AND IS MOSTLY ENGAGED IN SELF-GRATIFICATION. HANUMAN REPRESENTS THE EVOLUTION OF OUR MONKEY MINDS, AND OF THE FAITH, DEVOTION AND LOVE THAT GIVES US STRENGTH. HANUMAN FLIES ACROSS THE OCEAN TO BRING RAM'S RING TO SITA, AND SIGNAL THAT LOVE AND FAITH WILL RELEASE SITA FROM CAPTIVITY. HANUMAN FINDS HER AND RESTORES THE SHAKTI, FEMININE POWER, TO GOD, REUNITING RAM THE SUPREME AND SITA, OUR SOUL. HOPE STARTS THE JOURNEY, FAITH SUSTAINS IT, BUT IT ENDS BEYOND BOTH HOPE AND FAITH.

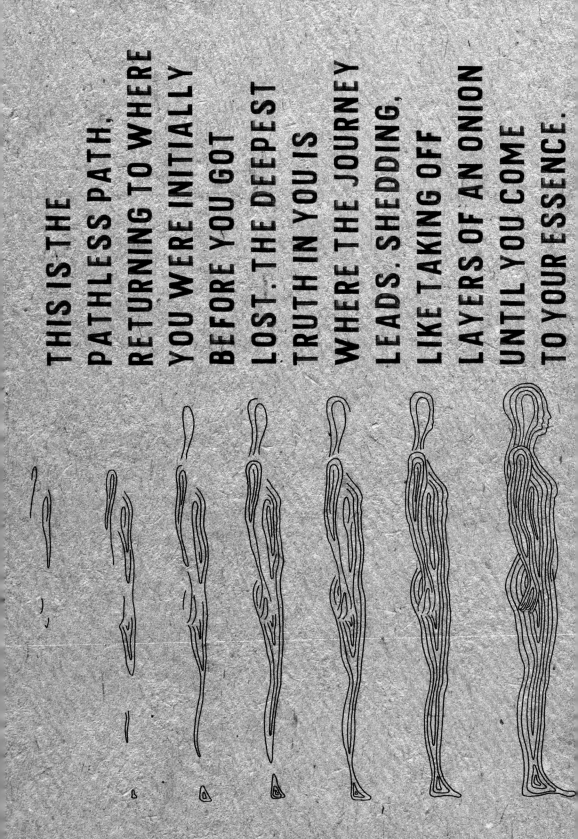

THIS IS THE PATHLESS PATH, RETURNING TO WHERE YOU WERE INITIALLY BEFORE YOU GOT LOST. THE DEEPEST TRUTH IN YOU IS WHERE THE JOURNEY LEADS. SHEDDING, LIKE TAKING OFF LAYERS OF AN ONION UNTIL YOU COME TO YOUR ESSENCE.

THE KEY TO THE SPIRITUAL JOURNEY IS NOT ACQUIRING SOMETHING OUTSIDE OF YOURSELF. RATHER IT IS SHEDDING THE VEILS TO COME BACK TO THE DEEPEST TRUTH OF YOUR BEING. ALL THAT YOU SEEK IS ALREADY WITHIN YOU.

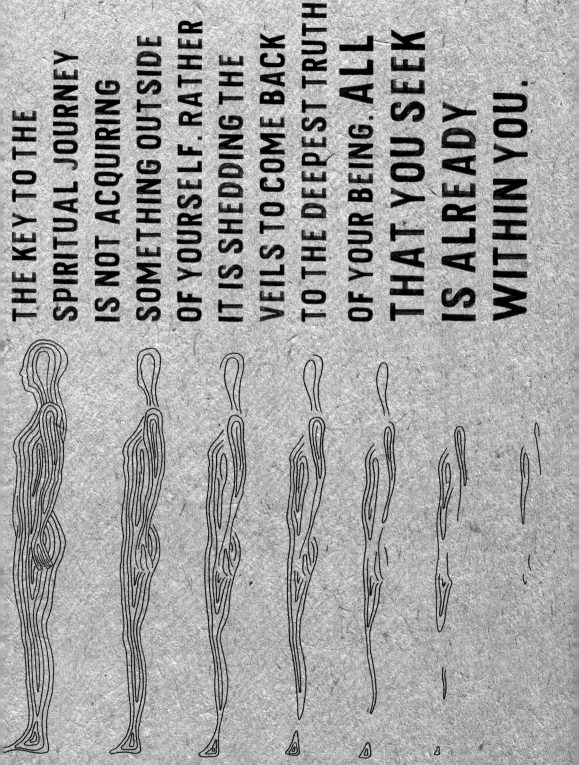

IT'S SO CLEAR THAT THE OBVIOUS, OPTIMUM STRATEGY

FOR IF THE WORLD IS GONNA END IN A MINUTE OR IF

IT'S GONNA END IN TEN BILLION YEARS IS TO BE CLEAR,

CONSCIOUS, PRESENT AND HERE. TO NOT BE PULLED

OR PUSHED OR FRIGHTENED OR GRABBING OR HOLDING.

YOU'RE JUST RIGHT HERE. AND THEN HERE.

AND THEN HERE. AND THEN, HERE. AND

THE OPTIMUM STRATEGY FOR YOU TO BE TOTALLY

PROCESSING EVERYTHING AND BE IN HARMONY WITH

THE NATURAL ORDER OF THE UNIVERSE IS TO **BE IN THE MOMENT. TO BE WITH THE MOMENT**, FULLY. WHICH INCLUDES THE PAST AND THE FUTURE. IT DOESN'T NEGATE IT. IT'S ALL IN HERE, THE PRESENT. WHILE WE SHARE THE OVERALL JOURNEY, EVERYONE'S PARTICULAR EXPERIENCES ARE THEIR OWN. THE EXPERIENCES ALONG THE WAY ARE NOT ENLIGHTENMENT. EVEN IF YOU DON'T FEEL THE GREATEST PEACE, OR EVEN IF NOTHING SEEMS TO BE HAPPENING, DON'T COMPARE OR JUDGE. JUST KEEP GOING. **PRESENT IN EACH MOMENT.**

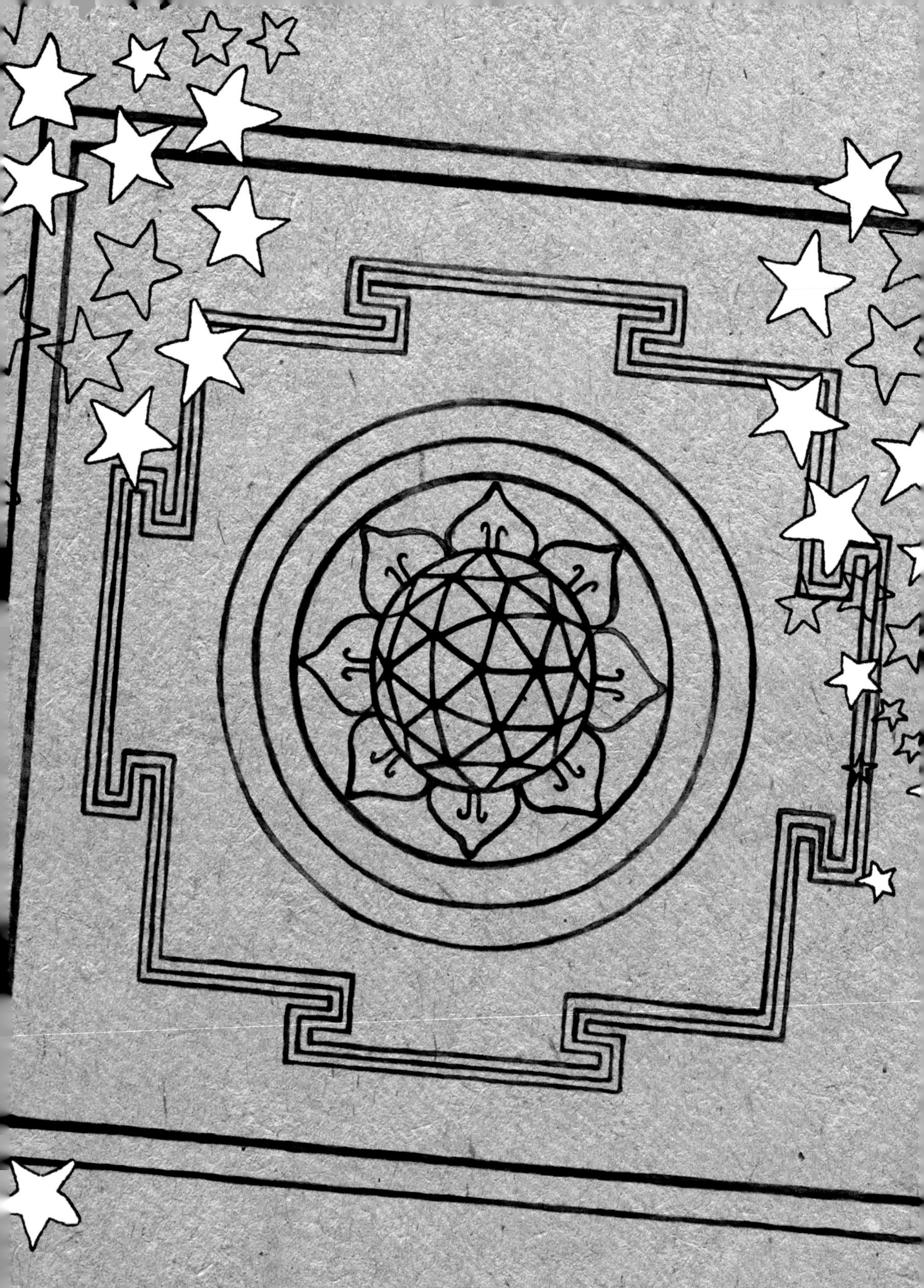

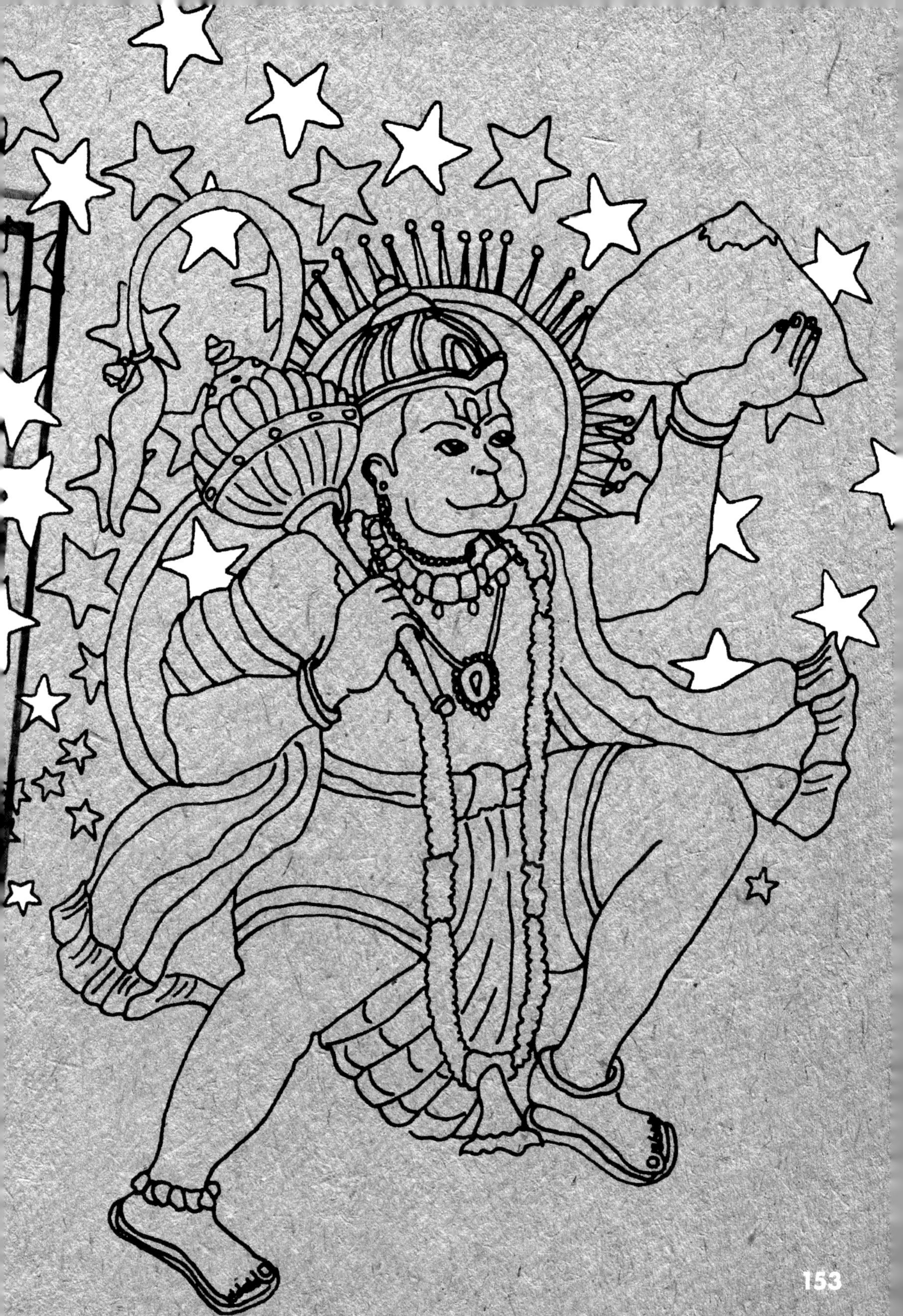

SECTION THREE

THE
TOOLBOX

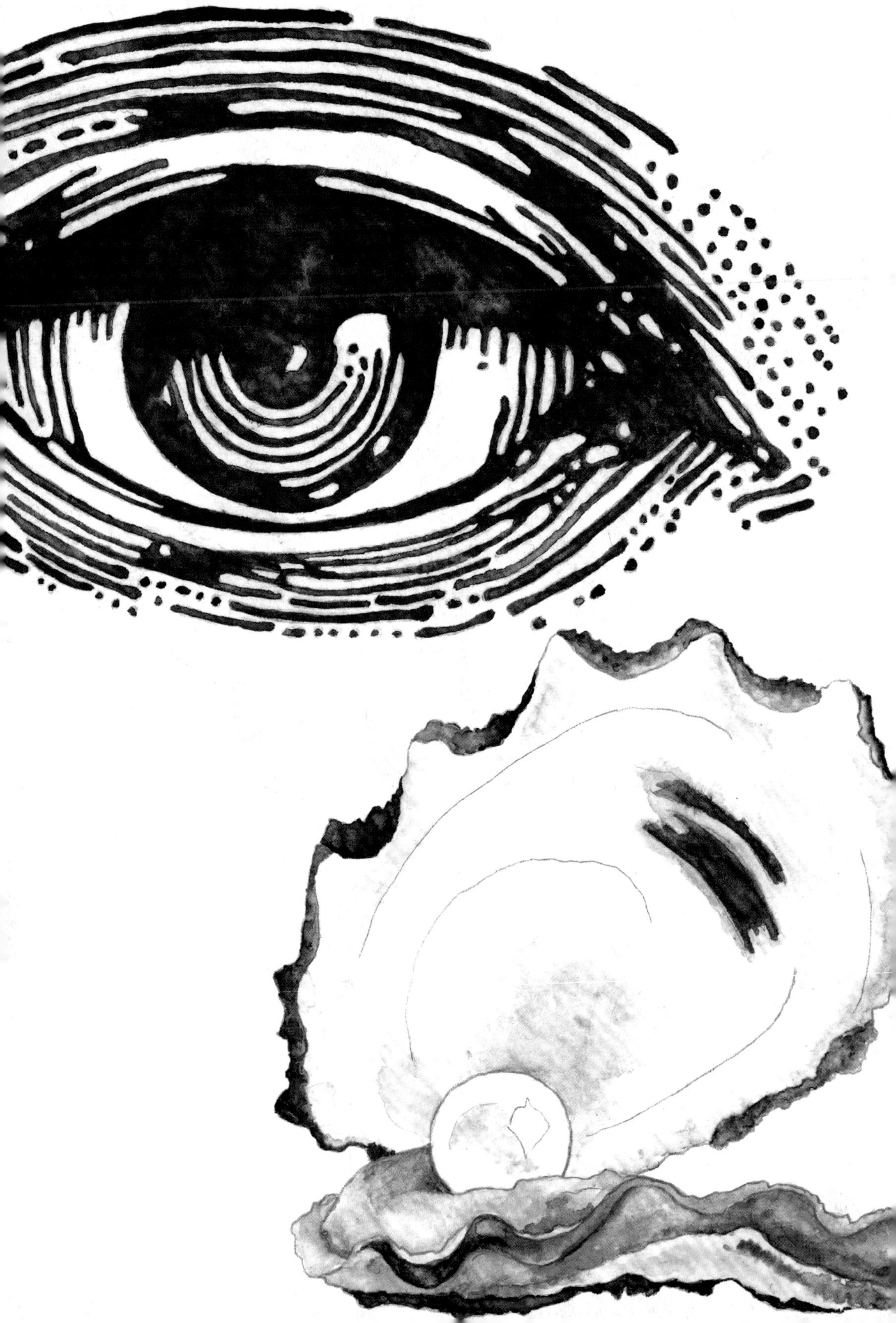

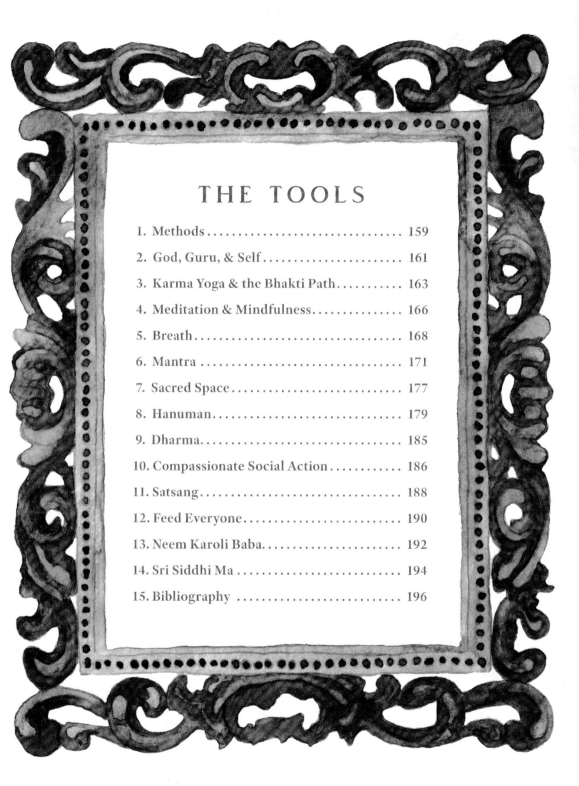

THE TOOLS

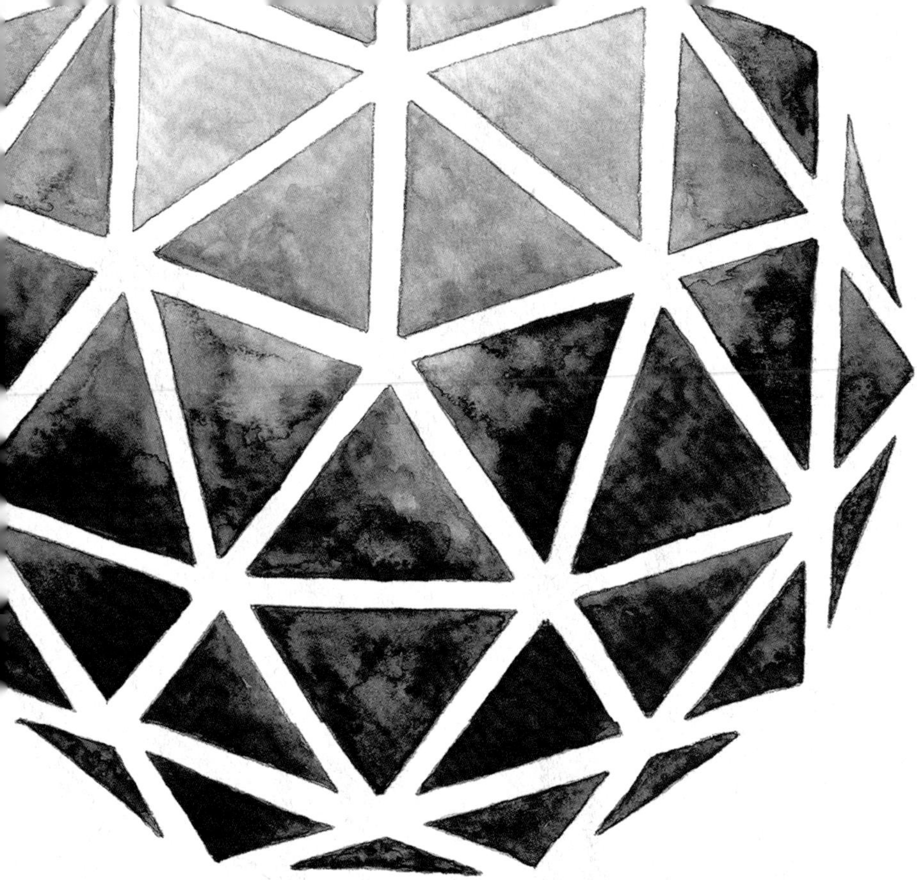

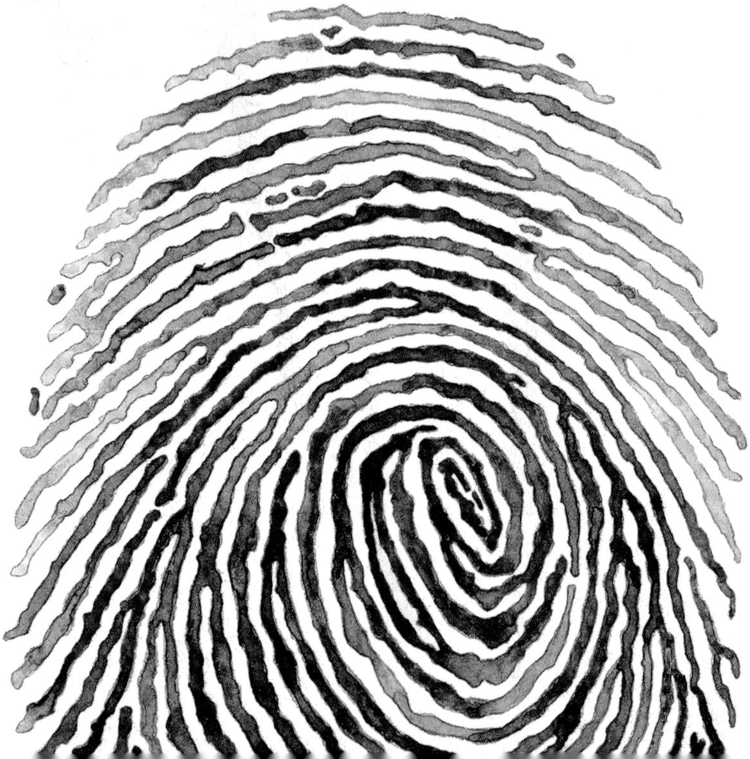

METHODS

Meditation is a method. Devotion and prayer are methods. Hatha yoga is a method. Dance is a method. Methods upon methods. However, the methods are an illusion. You use the illusion to get out of the illusion.

Transformation that comes from various spiritual practices is a spiral, a cycle. At times in my life I worked with external methods, such as service. At other times the pull was inward and I retreated from society to spend more time alone. The timing for these phases in the spiral must be in tune with your inner voice and your outer life.

THERE ARE MANY METHODS TO CHOOSE FROM TO HELP YOU GAIN INNER FREEDOM AND CONNECT TO A HIGHER CONSCIOUSNESS. And which do you pursue? You must listen quietly inside. Don't pick something because it's the hip thing to do. It doesn't work that way. Look around and see what methods you feel might be most useful to you.

If your mind is agitated and you need to calm your mind down, look around for meditation techniques. Learn how to meditate and you'll learn how to quiet the mind. If your heart is tight and closed, approach devotional yogas and techniques. If you feel that you don't understand what's been happening to you, study some philosophy and you'll begin to understand what the game is all about. If you find that you're tuning to spaces where huge amounts of energy are pouring through you and your body is weak, get your diet straight. Learn to sit tall so that energy can flow freely through you and you can become strong. You can become strong enough to hold all the energy of the universe, not to withstand it but to surrender into it.

So you work with one method after the next until all aspects – heart, mind, and body – are balanced. If you begin with one of them, sooner or later you will probably want to integrate the others as well. It makes no difference which technique you start with. Try to sense what you're ready for and what you need. Above all, be honest with yourself.

Every individual's karma is unique to that individual. Your method, your *upaya*, must be found for your particular karma. You can't buy into someone else's trip. People come to me and say, "I went with this swami or this baba or this school or this discipline and they were beautiful people and I tried and nothing happened. Am I wrong?" They say, "It didn't feel right." And I say, "Always trust your inner voice."

Pick a method that feels right and do it for two weeks. At the end of two weeks, you're free to evaluate the method. Or give yourself three months or six months, or more. Don't get too rigidly attached to any single method. Turn to others when their time comes, when you are ready for them. Be careful. Methods are not the thing itself; methods can be traps. Every method. The guru, chanting, study, meditation, practices, all of it. Are all methods to be avoided? It doesn't seem so, but it does seem useful to see them in perspective. If you feel free only when you meditate, you're not really free. Freedom doesn't come from turning your back on your responsibilities. Methods are ships crossing the ocean of existence. If you're halfway across the sea, it's a little silly to decide methods are a bummer if you don't know how to swim. But once you get to the far shore, it would be silly to keep carrying your boat because there is no more water.

Plunge in. You need discipline to persist when the going gets rough or uncertain, and you need faith.

GOD, GURU, AND SELF

Everything, everything, everything, is composed of love. God is in everything, and God is consciousness, and love. Just love. God is everywhere. God is just where you are at the moment, and each of us has God within. Everyone you meet is God, who has come to teach you something. Maharajji said, "The best form in which to worship God is all forms." You begin to see that everybody and everything in the universe becomes your teacher.

You probably walked right by your guru. She may have stopped you and given you a traffic ticket. You probably didn't even give him a quarter when he was asking for a handout. The next true being of Buddha nature you meet may appear as a bus driver, a doctor, a weaver, an insurance salesperson, a musician, a chef, a teacher, or any of the thousands of roles that are required in a complex society. Do you think the guru's going to be someone with light streaming out, wearing a sign that says "I am your guru"? When you're ready to see, you'll see your guru. You will know them because the simple interaction between you will strengthen your faith in the holiness in humans. It's as simple as that.

A Guru is like a perfect mirror for oneself, so that when you're with them you only see your own stuff; that's all you see, you don't see your stuff mixed with their stuff, because they don't have any stuff. Since they themselves are not attached to being anybody, who you see them to be is merely your own projection. Being around such a being allows you to see the way in which you are creating the universe. That mirror helps you gain the perception of your own attachments, which ultimately allows you to become unattached to any models you have of the universe. My guru was a mirror that was showing me my own beauty. The guru is none other than God, who is none other than self, which is the unmanifest, absolute.

A teacher is a little different. With the teacher, you never know what you're getting, because part of what you see is their stuff and part of it is your stuff. You can certainly pick very prominent teachers. I mean, I'm a teacher, obviously. I give talks and lectures and write books. I'm not a guru, but I'm a teacher, and the only way you know a teacher is by your intuitive heart. My suggestion is that the only thing you owe a teacher is for you to get yourself free. You don't owe a teacher loyalty. A lot of them say, "Well, I've been teaching you, now support me or take care of me, or sign and promise me you will be my student," and I think that's all nonsense. I think you should take what you can from every teacher, and then go on.

I think that the idea should be to focus on teachings not teachers. All I know is when I need a teaching of some sort I go toward somebody who's teaching that, and I take the teaching, and I keep taking the part of that which feels intuitively right with my own heart. I do not take any teaching from somebody that goes against my own heart. I must trust that more than I must trust somebody else telling me what I need.

You may hear someone say, "surrender to God or guru." *Surrender* is an interesting word. When I say I'm surrendering to my guru, I'm not surrendering to that man; I'm surrendering to the God within that man, to the One and to love. And so for me it's not hard to surrender to that, to the light, to pure energy, to pure love.

My guru said, "I am always in communion with you." And I deeply understood that to be the case and in fact, that's who he became for me. When I talk about my method being *guru kripa*, meaning grace of the guru, it means that his consciousness is present with me all the time. He is a being who is with me always, and sometimes he's with me so closely that I am him. And this reminds me of the higher truth that GOD, GURU, AND SELF TRULY ARE ONE.

KARMA YOGA &
THE BHAKTI PATH

Yoga is a Sanskrit word based on the root word *yuj*, meaning to unite. Yoga is a method that originated in ancient India for creating a union between the mind, body, and spirit with universal consciousness and for liberation. The yoga I'm referring to is the union or merging of one's true self with the idea of true reality. IN KARMA YOGA AND BHAKTI YOGA, DEVOTIONAL SERVICE IS ONE OF THE KEY PLAYERS. Devotion means having a strong love or loyalty to someone or something. Devotional service is serving as an expression of your love and loyalty to someone or something. I feel that service is one of the most beautiful spiritual paths. The relationship between karma yoga and bhakti yoga is that they are both methods for merging into wholeness with All that is.

In the simplest sense you could say that karma yoga, or the path of action, is using your karma, or the stuff of your life, as a way of coming into union with however you define God, with your true self, with the universe, and as a devotional offering. Karma yoga is usually used to selflessly work in the world for the benefit of others. It's taking the things you do every day and making those actions into a sacred offering without attachments to the results of the actions.

So in that sense it has a devotional quality to it because you're offering your actions in honor of whatever or whoever you're devoted to. And you do your seva or service without desire for rewards, fame, or privilege. Any kind of service you do in a community or a family can be karma yoga, like when you're changing a diaper, when you're feeding, when you're loving, when you're dealing with a scraped knee, when you're supporting somebody by just being there with them. And so it's an attitude that one has. It's an attitude of offering, and it's an attitude of seeing how the actions you're performing are more than just merely performing actions. There are different ways that this works. It can work in a devotional sense, where I do whatever I'm doing as my offering to Maharajji. This is my karma yoga. I'm doing whatever I'm doing as I serve, but it's also an offering to him. And that's also working on myself. Do you hear all of those components of that?

I can also do karma yoga without the devotional component, but do it from a meditative point of view, called meditation in action. For example, when I'm washing a pot, I don't wash the pot as the devotional offering to something or someone specific, but rather I just come into the process of washing the pot until I'm fully in the moment. And I quiet my mind into washing the pot, very focused and meditatively, until there is merging with just washing-of-pot-ness going on. And that is also karma yoga. So karma yoga is taking the stuff you do every day and making it a devotional and/or meditative practice that brings you into union with All that is, into oneness.

Whether your method is devotional or meditative or both, karma yoga is seeing life as it is, the universe as it is, and then asking in what way is this the vehicle for bringing me back into balance in the universe so that I am more consciously part of all of it. Like if you have children, then children become your vehicle; if you have cancer, then cancer becomes your vehicle; if you have a family member that's a complete mess, then that family member becomes your vehicle; if you're living in an ecologically decaying universe, then that becomes your vehicle. Instead of seeing all these things as obstacles on your path, you see them as the path itself. Karma yoga was a way in which I could make living sacred. I tried to turn my path of action in the world into a sacred act of serving God in every moment. For me, that's what karma yoga is.

I'm also a bhakti yogi, and a bhakti yogi or yogini goes up the spiritual path by love. The *Ramayana* describes bhakti yoga as the easy way for a dark time, which you've noticed is getting darker. Bhakti yoga is a method for experiencing unity and harmony between the individual and the universal. Bhakti yoga is the yoga of the heart. It's a path of love. You're loving your God, you're loving your guru; love of yourself, love of your fellow humans, you're loving.

As bhakti yogis, we focus on the divine with our mind, emotions, and senses. Our loving devotion is the path for spirituality that includes many methods. We include kirtan, which is singing mantra and different names describing God. And the music and kirtan is one form of getting to God, by merging with the mantra, and the sounds, chanting, vibrations and the moment. We also get together. That's called satsang. That's pretty bhakti. We discuss Hanuman and his devotion and service. That's pretty bhakti. And service is another method that we discuss and do together. That's very bhakti. Another component is the guru and guru kripa, which is the grace of the guru. That is bhakti. Guru kripa means that no matter what I'm doing, I'm doing it all to honor my guru. Then we discuss the path of love. That's certainly bhakti. Bhakti is going towards the One, with the heart. So all these components are bhakti. It's a path of the heart. Through the heart. Because that's the essence of the bhakti path. So I see bhakti or devotion yoga is at the level of the soul, basically.

That's how I did bhakti and karma yoga, but you can do it differently.

MEDITATION &
MINDFULNESS

It can be useful to have a kind of daily practice just to keep bringing you back into the moment, to help slow your mind down, create greater self-awareness, and become more mindful. A regular meditative practice brings you back to a neutral place, the witness perspective, clear and present, just mindful in the moment. It's like clearing a computer, like pushing the delete button. Meditation just erases all the junk for that moment, and the regularity is important, especially when you're bored and you don't want to do it because that's the way the ego is.

MEDITATION RAISES THE QUESTION,

"Who am I really?"

Your ego is a set of thoughts that define your universe. It is like a familiar room built of thoughts; you see the universe through its windows. The ego will do everything it can to keep you being just who you always were. The ego wants to preserve itself, and by using methods like meditation, mindfulness, mantra, and service, you are very slowly, slowly realizing who you are.

Initially most people choose to meditate out of curiosity or to relieve psychological pain, increase pleasure, or enhance power. The goal of all these motives is to strengthen the ego. As the ego gets more comfortable, happy, and powerful, it tempts you into becoming self-involved in your mindfulness practices.

The ego's motives don't allow examination of the ego itself, nor do they allow insight that the ego is restricting. These motives paradoxically contain the seeds of freedom, because they lead you to meditate more. As your meditation develops beyond the level of ego payoffs, you will experience an opening.

The more I center myself and meditate, the more I hear how it all is. If there's an uneven place in me, that's where I have to work on myself. While we cannot avoid the difficult challenges of life, how we deal with an experience can magnify or reduce their impact. Thoughts, emotions, and sensations come up constantly that disturb my heart and mind. Though I may get angry, I let go of the anger more quickly. And more importantly, I let go of the guilt connected with the anger.

With meditation, these feelings now simply arise and pass away, without my resisting or clinging to them. More and more I am just awareness. The explanation is involvement without clinging, not grabbing at anything. The final step in integrating meditation into your awareness is to use the stuff of daily life as part of your meditation, so that each experience brings you more deeply into the meditative space. Meditation will help you quiet your mind, enhance your ability to be insightful and understanding, and give you a sense of inner peace.

Be open to whatever experiences come in your meditation. Don't get fixated on a model of what meditation is supposed to feel like. Set aside judging, being critical, having opinions. Meditation is giving up models and labels. There is no best or right kind of experience in meditation; each session is as different and unique as each day of your life. Twenty minutes per day of meditation practice can lead to noticeable results and the incentive to go deeper still. Continuous practice brings about great transformation of mind and leads to a new quality of service. I've found that each meditation technique I've ever pursued seriously has helped me by experiencing another space in my being. Somehow I've danced through them without getting caught in a value system that would say that a single meditative technique is the only way. The game isn't to end up a good meditator, but to end up free. The game isn't to end up loving; it's to end up being love.

BREATH

Breathing is the single most important act that we do every day. It's very simple and natural. It's part of nature. The breath is always moving, but so is the mind. It's important to be aware of the breath, and not be so caught in the web of thoughts and the stuff of our experience.

The meditative technique I use, which is so Mickey Mouse it's absurd, is I follow the breath. It's an ancient technique. I follow the breath rising and falling in my abdomen. There's a little muscle that goes up and down when you breathe. You can feel it, if you place your hands on your diaphragm, just below your lungs and heart. The instruction from my teacher was, "Follow the breath. Follow the rising and the falling. When it rises, notice that it's rising, and when it's falling, notice it falling."

When you're ready to meditate, close your eyes and bring your attention to the motion of your breath as it enters and leaves your nostrils. Keep your focus at the nostrils, noting the full passage of each in-breath and out-breath from beginning to end. Now don't follow the breath into your lungs or out into the air; just watch its flow in and out of the nostrils. If you can, notice the subtle sensations of the breath as it comes and goes. Be aware of each inhalation and exhalation as it passes by the nostrils, just as the doorman watches each person who comes and goes through a door.

Attend to the feeling of the breath. Don't try to imagine it or visualize it. Note the sensation of the breath just as it is, exactly as you feel it. You may feel the breath at the rim of the nostrils, or just inside the nose, or on the upper lip beneath the nose. The sensations you feel will change. You may sometimes feel the breath like the light touch of a feather, like a dull throb, or as an intense point of pressure on your lip, or in countless other ways. There is no right way for the breath to feel. Just be aware of what it is. EACH TIME YOU NOTICE YOUR MIND HAS WANDERED TO OTHER THOUGHTS, OR IS CAUGHT BY BACKGROUND NOISES, BRING YOUR ATTENTION BACK TO THE EASY, NATURAL RHYTHM OF YOUR BREATHING.

Don't try to control your breath. Simply watch it. Fast or slow, shallow or deep, the nature of the breath does not matter. Your full attention to it is what counts.

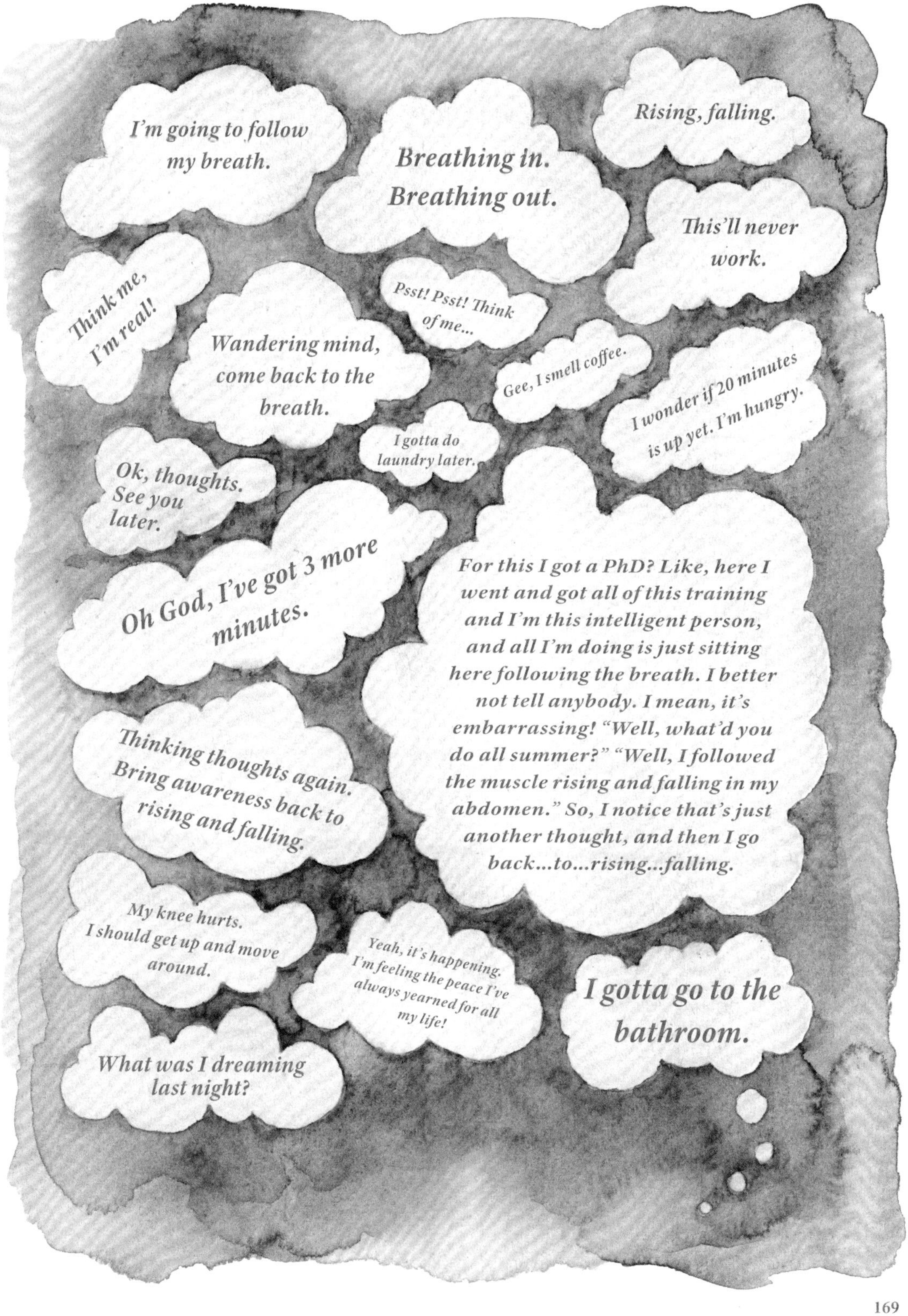
I'm going to follow my breath.
Breathing in. Breathing out.
Rising, falling.
This'll never work.
Think me, I'm real!
Psst! Psst! Think of me...
Wandering mind, come back to the breath.
Gee, I smell coffee.
I wonder if 20 minutes is up yet. I'm hungry.
I gotta do laundry later.
Ok, thoughts. See you later.
Oh God, I've got 3 more minutes.
For this I got a PhD? Like, here I went and got all of this training and I'm this intelligent person, and all I'm doing is just sitting here following the breath. I better not tell anybody. I mean, it's embarrassing! "Well, what'd you do all summer?" "Well, I followed the muscle rising and falling in my abdomen." So, I notice that's just another thought, and then I go back...to...rising...falling.
Thinking thoughts again. Bring awareness back to rising and falling.
My knee hurts. I should get up and move around.
Yeah, it's happening. I'm feeling the peace I've always yearned for all my life!
I gotta go to the bathroom.
What was I dreaming last night?

Now, what a simple exercise like that does, which is just a mechanical method without any religious overlay, is allow you to see the way in which your thoughts keep capturing you into being identified with them. Just doing that simple little exercise allows you to see your thoughts grabbing and taking you, until pretty soon you begin to see that the thoughts are an ocean of continuous thinking. It's like sitting on the edge of a stream and watching the water go by. Leaves come, and little fish go by, and all kinds of twigs and things go by. Every now and then something catches your consciousness and your head turns to follow it. When you're meditating you just keep it right there and the stuff comes in, exists, and goes by. What happens just from that little mechanical method is you start to develop a connection to the awareness. It's like the sky that's behind the clouds. To define who you are: You are just awareness.

Your mind becomes a field of awareness. All your thoughts become phenomena. All the sensations as well, and the awareness keeps turning back in on itself until what is left is not the experience of emptiness, but just emptiness and clarity, while all of the other planes of the experience are still present.

If you have trouble keeping your mind on the breath, count each breath up to ten, then start over again at one. Or, to anchor your mind on your breath, you can occasionally make a strong, deliberate inhalation and exhalation. Then let your breath return to its normal rate. Whenever you realize you're thinking about something else, return your awareness to your breath.

Don't try to fight off thoughts. Just let them go. If sounds distract you, do the same. Let them be and simply start watching your breath again. If aches or itches bother you, slowly move or shift to ease them if you must. But keep your mind on breathing while you do it. Just keep returning your attention to your breath, letting go of whatever the mind wanders to. THIS IS THE ESSENCE OF MEDITATION: LETTING GO OF YOUR THOUGHTS.

MANTRA

A mantra could be a word, sound, a name of God, or a spiritual phrase that is repeated over and over again. The practice of mantra is an effective way to concentrate your mind, and keep your consciousness centered. But as important as it is to concentrate your mind, what you concentrate on is equally as important. Although the mind can focus on anything, only certain words can qualify as a mantra. A mantra must connect you with the sacred and allows each moment to become the moment of awakening. It allows each moment to be

the moment.

There are all different kinds of mantras. Some mantras are personal, that which you don't share with anyone. There are general mantras, and mantras for developing great powers. It's an absolutely unbeatable technique for getting high. Wherever you are, mantras take you to another plane.

Let yourself into the chant just as if you were getting into a hot tub. Don't just dive in. Don't just get a blissful smile on your face and start to intone it. If you start from the wrong place it'll be hard to get it straight. Let it suck you in. Just start really slow.

When you first start to say a mantra, you're hearing it outside through your ears, saying it, chanting or singing it aloud, and thinking about its meaning. THE IDEA OF A MANTRA IS THAT IT REPEATS OVER AND OVER AGAIN, RELEASING YOUR ATTACHMENT TO ALL OTHER THOUGHTS, UNTIL THEY ARE LIKE BIRDS GLIDING BY. It's a training device to help break you out of your attachments.

It's putting one set of thoughts into your head in place of another set of thoughts. In other words, the mantra is a technique for bringing us into a place in ourselves that would be called the eternal present. This is a place where nothing is literally happening at all. It's simply a device for calming our minds.

Once the mantra has been going on for a while, it starts to change in its nature. You stop thinking about what it means. You just sort of get absorbed in the sound of it. Then the mantra starts to move into your head, and then moves down into your chest, until pretty soon it's going around like a little wheel, going around inside your chest.

At that point you've stopped focusing on its meaning. Now it's got another quality to it, taking on a kind of vibration or harmony with the universe in a certain way. The sounds of languages, like Sanskrit, are connected with various states of consciousness. If you repeat them over and over again, they will take you to a certain state of consciousness.

You don't have to chant it out loud. In fact, you can just listen to it and let yourself just fall into it.

Keep remembering the mantra, even while you're going about the business of your day. Invite it to stay with you. You can coordinate the mantra with your steps as you walk or with any rhythmic activity. No matter what else you do, keep doing the mantra. You will reach a point where instead of you chanting the mantra, the mantra is chanting you.

Here are a few of my favorite mantras:

OM MANI PADME HUM

OM MANI PADME HUM, a Tibetan mantra, is one of the most widely used mantras in the world today. In fact, in Nepal you'll see rocks twenty feet long and ten feet high with *OM MANI PADME HUM* written in tiny letters all over the whole rock, so you can just read it like a letter. And there are prayer wheels at the temples where written in them ten million times is the phrase *OM MANI PADME HUM*, and you see lamas going around stupas saying *"OM MANI PADME HUM."*

There are many meanings. One of the ways of understanding its meaning is that *OM* is a sacred sound considered by many to be an unlimited and eternal sound of the universe. It means *Brahma* or *atman*, that which is behind it all, the entirety of the universe, the unmanifest, and that which is beyond form. *MANI* means the All is the jewel or crystal. *PADME* means lotus, and *HUM* means heart. So on one level what it means is the entire universe is just like a pure jewel or crystal right in the heart or center of the lotus flower, which is me, and it's manifest in the center of my heart, it's manifest light, residing in my own heart. That's one way of interpreting it.

You start to say *OM MANI PADME HUM* and you're thinking, "God, in unmanifest form, is like a jewel in the middle of a lotus, manifest in my heart." You go through that and feel it in your heart. The All or God is the jewel in the center of the lotus, manifest in my heart. God is the jewel in the center of the lotus which is nothing else but my heart. And you keep repeating that, *OM MANI PADME HUM*, starting the *OM* around your belly button, but back in your spine, and you imagine bringing it up your spine with *OM MANI PADME* and then pouring it into your heart with the *HUM*. And keep going that way.

Remember, bring it up the spine, pour it into the heart. You breathe in on the *OM*. You can do three or four *OM MANI PADME HUM* repetitions with one breath. Just very naturally.

राम राम राम राम राम राम

RAMA RAM

राम I came back from India, chanting the mantra that my Guru was constantly
repeating, "*RAM, RAM, RAM, RAM, RAM, RAM, RAM...*" *Rama* (rhymes with
mama,) or *Ram* (rhymes with *mom*) is another name for God, or consciousness,
or oneness, or love. Rama is the devoted husband of Sita, and the divine mas-
राम culine form of God. Ram in the spiritual classic the *Ramayana* represents the राम
forces of consciousness and love. He's the perfect balance of devotion, compassion, wisdom and power. Ram is the essence of who you are when you realize राम
your true self.

Another way to chant this mantra is, "*SITA RAM, SITA RAM, SITA RAM,
SITA RAM.*" Sita, Ram's devoted wife, is the divine feminine form of God and
creative life force. She is known for her perfect balance of self-sacrifice, bravery,
purity, and dedication to *Ram.*

राम "*SITA RAMA, SITA RAMA, SITA RAMA.*" Say it, think it, feel it in your heart. राम
When you chant this mantra, you are continually meeting and merging into the
perfect balance of Sita and Ram.

174

THE POWER OF GOD IS WITHIN ME, THE GRACE OF GOD SURROUNDS ME

This is a mantra that you can use whenever you're frightened about forces affecting you. It's a mantra that creates what feels like a solid steel beam that goes from above through the top of your head right down through your middle to the base of your being. It's like a shield, an impenetrable egg around you. And the mantra is

"THE POWER OF GOD IS WITHIN ME, THE GRACE OF GOD SURROUNDS ME."

You've got to feel it as you say it. Just let yourself feel it, as if the power of God pours down into you as a strong force, like a steel core, and then you're surrounded by a shield. Grace will surround you like a force field, but don't make the grace too heavy, because it's like a very fine protective mist around you so that you're not hardened toward the world and can respond to evil with love. Create this protective device and then send love. That's what the mist is; it's a mist of love and grace. It just radiates out from you, but doesn't let anything in.

175

I AM
LOVING AWARENESS

This is a meditation where you focus your mind on a point in the heart space, in the middle of the chest, and say, "I AM LOVING AWARENESS. I AM LOVING AWARENESS. I AM LOVING AWARENESS."

You were identifying with ego, and this mantra can help you become the reality of your true self. As you sink into this practice, you might think, "I can do without this, this will never work, this is crap," but that's the ego talking.

Keep repeating to yourself, "*I AM LOVING AWARENESS. I AM LOVING AWARENESS.*" Remember to mentally focus your attention in the middle of the chest. You're going to make loving awareness the pivot point of your consciousness. In the future, you'll know yourself as loving awareness. If somebody asks you your name, of course, you don't say, "I am loving awareness," but you will say this to yourself. While walking down the street or going into the grocery store, say, "*I AM LOVING AWARENESS.*" Now take on that identity instead of the identity you had before. You shift your identity to "I am loving awareness." The awareness is not an objective thing. You can't point to awareness. You're aware of your eyes seeing, you're aware of your ears hearing, you're aware of your thoughts as they come out of your mind. So "this will never work" is a thought, and just label it as a thought. Label thoughts. This loving awareness is the witness of your incarnation.

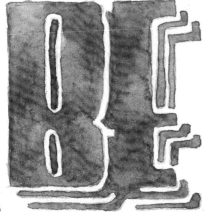 

SACRED SPACE

In India, worship is called puja, and a puja table or puja room is a sacred space for doing conscious work on yourself, like meditation, worship, prayer, reading holy books, reflection, centering, or doing mantra or chanting. It's a place for remembering your true self, or just a source of spiritual comfort. It can be a space for doing devotional rituals or for burning candles and incense, offering food, or just hanging out.

You can create small altars or shrines at your desk or in your computer space, in your room, at the entryway of your home, or on the door of the refrigerator. Create a sanctuary in the garden, at your doorstep, on the patio or deck, or on the dashboard of your car.

You can customize your space. Keep it simple yet personalized. YOUR SACRED ALTAR HONORS YOUR HIGHEST SELF, CONNECTING YOU TO THE INFINITE. Pictures of loved

ones you wish to bless, artwork, poetry or prayers for family, friends or even enemies who are suffering or sick, may help open everyone's heart. You can decorate your puja table with statues, flowers, fruit, beautiful stones or shells, or anything you find beautiful or meaningful.

See these objects as reflections of your own beauty and your interconnection to the natural world. Let these images and objects inspire and center you into the present moment. Your puja table occupies your heart and mind, and connects you to your true self. Carry this energy with you throughout the day. Know that you can never have too many sacred spaces.

Let spirit permeate your life. Spiritualize your life from the outside, but know the real work is within.

HANUMAN

I want to introduce you to the monkey Hanuman, one of the central characters in Hindu texts like the *Ramayana* and the *Mahabhurata*. IIc's the son of the brave Kesari and heroic Anjani, and also known as the son of Vaya, the god of wind, because of his role in Hanuman's birth. He's sometimes referred to as *Sankata Mochan*, the remover of obstacles, sorrow and suffering. HANUMAN COMBINES HIS FEARLESS POWER, INTELLIGENCE AND STRENGTH WITH KARMA AND BHAKTI YOGA, TO LOVE AND SERVE GOD IN THE FORM OF RAM. That's why he's sometimes shown as kneeling.

Hanuman and I would meditate together. He strengthened in me my own courage, devotion, and dedication to serve. People thought of Maharajji as an incarnation of Hanuman, because he was also about love, service and devotion. Because of my guru, we honor Hanuman. I tried to be like Hanuman and become those qualities, and live up to my namesake. I think Hanuman is teaching us that the *siddhis*, or powers, come from love. And I think Hanuman teaches us quiet, solidness, and peace.

The *Hanuman Chalisa* is a powerful poem, written in the sixteenth century by a poet and saint named Tulsidas. This *chalise,* or forty verse devotional chant, is said or sung as a way to honor Hanuman, and remind us that we, too, can embody the qualities that Hanuman personifies, and to ask for Hanuman's blessing. It strengthens our devotion, infuses us with joy and positive energy, bhakti, strength, confidence and courage. It is also said that chanting the *Chalisa* helps one gain spiritual wisdom, overcome fears, bring protection and ward off evil, gain good health, remove all obstacles, and bring other blessings for good fortune.

Maharajji loved the *Hanuman Chalisa* and said, "Every line of the *Hanuman Chalisa* is a *maha* mantra, or greatest mantra."

SHRĪ HANUMĀN CHĀLĪSĀ

(from Prayers of Love From Kainchi Dham by Prarthna Priti)

*maṅgala mūrati māruta nandana
sakala amaṅgala mūla nikandana*

Son of the Wind, embodiment of blessings and joy, you destroy the root of all that is inauspicious.

*shrī guru charaṇ saroja raja nija
mana mukura sudhāri
baraṇau raghubara bimala jasu jo
dāyaka phala chāri*

Having polished the mirror of my heart with the dust from my Guru's lotus feet, I sing the pure fame of the best of Raghus, which bestows the four fruits of life.

*buddhihīna tanu jānike sumiraü
pavana kumār
bala buddhi vidyā dehu mohī harahu
kalesha bikār*

I know I have no intelligence, I recall the Son of the Wind. Please give me strength, intelligence, and wisdom and remove my suffering and impurities.

*siyā vara rāmachandra pada jaya
sharanam*

Hail to the refuge of the feet of Sita's husband, Ramachandra.

*1. jaya hanumāna jñāna guṇa sāgar
jaya kapīsa tihū loka ujāgar*

Glory to you Hanuman, ocean of wisdom and virtue. Hail to the Lord of the Monkeys, the illuminator of the three worlds.

*2. rāma dūta atulita bala dhāmā
añjani putra pavanasuta nāmā*

Ram's emissary, abode of matchless power, Anjani's son, named Son of the Wind.

*3. mahābīra bikrama bajaraṅgī
kumati nivāra sumati ke saṅgī*

Great hero, mighty as a thunderbolt, remover of negative thoughts and companion to the good.

*4. kañchana barana birāja subesā
kānana kuṇḍala kuñchita kesa*

Golden hued and splendidly adorned
with heavy earrings and curly locks.

5. *hātha vajra au dhvajā birājai*
kāṅdhe mūnja jane-ū sājai

In your hands shine mace and a ban-
ner; a sacred thread of munja grass
adorns your shoulder.

6. *shaṅkara suvana kesarī nandana*
teja pratāpa mahā jaga bandana

You are Siva's incarnation and Kesari's
son – your glory is renowned throughout the world.

7. *vidyāvāna guṇī ati chātura*
rāma kāja karibe ko ātura

You are the supremely wise, virtuous,
and clever. You are ever intent on
Ram's work.

8. *prabhu charitra sunibe ko rasiyā*
rāma lakhana sītā mana basiyā

You delight in hearing of the Lord's
deeds. Ram, Lakshman, and Sita dwell
in your heart.

9. *sūkshma rūpa dhari siyahī dikhāvā*
bikaṭa rūpa dhari laṅka jarāvā

Assuming a tiny form you appeared
to Sita, and in awesome guise you
burned Lanka.

10. *bhīma rūpa dhari asura saṅhāre*
rāmachandraji ke kāja saṅvāre

Taking a dreadful form, you slaugh-
tered the demons and completed Lord
Ram's mission.

11. *lāya sajīvana lakhana jiyāye*
shrī raghubīra harashi ura lāye

Bringing the life-giving sajivana herb,
you revived Lakshman, and Shri Ram
joyfully embraced you.

12. *raghupati kīnhī bahuta baṛā-ī*
tuma mama priya bharatahi sama bhā-ī

Greatly did the Lord of Raghus praise
you saying, "You are as dear to me as
my brother Bharat."

13. *sahasa badana tumharo jasa gāvaĩ*
asa kahi shrīpati kaṇṭha lagāvaĩ

"Thousands of mouths sing your
praise," so saying, Sita's Lord drew
you to himself.

14. *sanakādika brahmādi munīsā*
nārada shārada sahita ahīsā

Sanak and the sages, gods, Brahma,
great saints, Narada, Sharada, and
king of the serpents,

15. *yama kubera digapāla jahāṅ te*
kabi kobida kahi sake kahāṅ te

Yama, Kubera, and the guardians of the quadrants, poets and scholars – none can express your glory.

16. tuma upakāra sugrīvahī kīnhā
rāma milāya rājapada dīnhā

You rendered great service to Sugriva. Introducing him to Lord Ram, you gave him kingship.

17. tumharo mantra vibhīshana mānā
laṇkeshvara bha-e saba jaga jānā

Vibhishana heeded your counsel and became the lord of Lanka as all the world knows.

18. yuga sahasra yojana para bhānū
līlyo tāhi madhura phala jānū

Even though the sun is millions of miles away, you swallowed it, thinking it to be a sweet fruit.

19. prabhu mudrikā meli mukha māhīn
jaladhi lāṇghi gaye acharaja nāhīṅ

Holding the Lord's ring in your mouth, it is no surprise you leapt over the ocean.

20. durgama kāja jagata ke jete
sugama anugraha tumhare tete

Every arduous task in this world becomes easy by your grace.

21. rāma duāre tuma rakhavāre
hota na ājñā binu paisāre

You are the guardian at the door of Ram's abode, no one enters without your leave.

22. saba sukha lahai tumhārī sharanā
tuma rakshaka kāhū ko dara nā

Taking refuge in you, one finds complete contentment. Those you protect know no fear.

23. āpana teja samhārau āpai
tīnō loka hāṅka tē kāṅpai

You alone can withstand your own splendor. The three worlds tremble at your roar.

24. bhūta pisācha nikaṭa nahī āvai
mahābīra jaba nāma sunāvai

Ghosts and goblins cannot come near, great hero, when your name is uttered.

25. nāsai roga hare saba pīrā
japata nirantara hanumata bīrā

All disease and pain is eradicated by the constant repetition of your name.

26. saṅkaṭa se hanumāna chhuṛāvai
mana krama bachana dhyāna jo lāvai

Hanuman releases from affliction those who remember him in thought, word and deed.

27. *saba para rāma tapasvī rājā*
tina ke kāja sakala tuma sājā

Ram the renunciate king reigns over all. You carry out all his work.

28. *aura manoratha jo ko-ī lāvai*
so-ī amita jīvana phala pāvai

One who brings any yearning to you obtains the four fruits of life.

29. *chārõ yuga paratāpa tumhārā*
hai parasiddha jagata ujiyārā

Your splendor fills the four ages; your glory lights up the world.

30. *sādhu santa ke tuma rakhavāre*
asura nikandana rāma dulāre

You are the protector of saints and sages, the destroyer of demons, and the darling of Ram.

31. *ashṭa siddhi nau nidhi ke dātā*
asa bara dīna jānakī mātā

You grant the eight powers and the nine treasures by the boon you received from Mother Janaki [Sita].

32. *rāma rasāyana tūmhare pāsā*
sadā raho raghupati ke dāsā

You hold the elixir of Ram's name and are forever his servant.

33. *tumhare bhajana rāmajī ko pāvai*
janma janma ke duḥkha bisarāvai

Singing your praise, one finds Ram and the sorrows of lifetimes are left behind.

34. *anta kāla raghubara pura jā-ī*
jahāṅ janma hari-bhakta kahā-ī

At death one goes to Ram's own abode, born as God's devotee.

35. *aura devatā chitta na dhara-ī*
hanumata se-i sarva sukha kara-ī

There is no need to remember any other deity; worshiping Hanuman one gains all happiness.

36. *sankaṭa kaṭai miṭai saba pīrā*
jo sumirai hanumata bala bīrā

All suffering and pain vanish when one remembers the brave Hanuman.

37. *jai jai jai hanumāna gosā-ī*
kṛpā karahu gurudeva kī nā-ī

Glory, glory, glory to you Lord Hanuman. Bestow your grace on me as my Guru!

38. jo shata bāra pāṭha kara ko-ī
chhūṭahi bandi mahā sukha ho-ī

Whoever recites this 100 times is freed
from bondage and enjoys bliss.

39. jo yaha paṛe hanumāna chālīsā
hoya siddhi sākhī gaurīsā

Those who read this Hanuman Chalisa
gains abilities and success, as Gauri's
Lord (Siva) bears witness.

40. tulasīdāsa sadā hari cherā
kījai nātha hṛdaya mahā ḍerā

Says Tulsidas, Hari's constant servant,
"Lord, please make your home in my heart."

pavana tanaya saṅkaṭa harana maṅ-
gala mūrati rūpa
rāma lakhana sītā sahita hṛdaya
basahu sura bhūpa

Son of the Wind, king of gods, ban-
isher of sorrow and embodiment of
blessings, dwell in my heart together
with Ram, Lakshman, and Sita.

siyā vara rāmchandra pada jaya
sharanam

Hail to the refuge of the feet of Sita's
husband, Ramachandra.

DHARMA

Dharma is the way, or the path. It's the appropriate action or right way of living. It's the way in which we fulfill our moral duties. It brings you to truth, to God, or to oneness. Dharma brings you back into unity and out of the illusion of separateness.

EACH OF US HAS A UNIQUE DHARMA, PATH, OR WAY THROUGH TO OUR SOUL.

Maybe you already intuitively know this, but the game isn't that all of us become alike. Each of us is hearing a different message of what our specific path is. We've got to be very quiet to hear our own dharma, our unique way of acting compassionately. There's no rule book about this. Somebody comes along and their major thing is to awaken people to environmental destruction. Someone else comes along and their major thing is to end incredible inequality and oppression in the world, and so on. It isn't a question of which thing is worse, or which is more worthwhile.

Every individual contribution is to be honored. Each person has to hear their specific part. And no role is better than any other role. Whatever you're doing in your life is no better or worse than what I'm doing in my life. It's just different. Each of us has a unique route through, and the art isn't to imitate somebody else's route but to listen to hear our own route. The quieter and more conscious I became, the more my heart opened and I saw that I could make a more compassionate contribution toward the relief of suffering.

Understand that what you hear one moment may be different than what you hear a moment later and that it is constantly changing. There will be inconsistency, and there will also be everybody's expectations that you will be consistent. From a meditative space, you will hear the way your dharma is evolving.

COMPASSIONATE SOCIAL ACTION

It's very interesting how you help another human being. You can help them in such a way that even though you put food in their belly, you starve them psychologically. You can make them feel more helpless if you're helping because you think it makes you look good. On the other hand, if you see yourself as part of a process in the universe, in which you do your part and they do their part, then everyone gets helped. There are ways to empower people by recognizing that we are

All One.

SOCIAL ACTION AND SPIRITUAL WORK ARE NOT MUTUALLY EXCLUSIVE. THE CURRICULUM OF SEVA, MEANING SERVICE, PROVIDES US WITH INFORMATION ABOUT OUR STRENGTHS, AND WE DISCOVER HOW THESE CONTRIBUTE TO GENUINELY HELPFUL SERVICE.

When you respond from your human heart's point of view to another person suffering, and your heart is open, you experience incredible pain. So most people respond with their intellect and they pull away when they get in the presence of suffering because they can't handle it. However, if you keep your heart open it hurts like hell, because when you start to appreciate that they are us and not just them, you can't intellectualize it anymore, you can't pull away. We are concerned and feel for other people's suffering.

Compassion then becomes the ability to balance both the incredible pain and the ability to keep your heart open enough to act with equanimity or balance, where you're acknowledging it to be what it is, and at the same moment allowing your human heart that wants to do something about it to reach out to do so.

You start to realize that you can't take away all the world's suffering, while at the same moment there is a way in which you see that you are a part of the machine of healing and compassion. It's that balancing we're playing with. To me, life is joy, and the joy can include the service. Instead of the joy or the service, it's the joy through the service; it's all of it.

I'm sure it's obvious to you, when you think about it, that the nature of your reference group has a lot to do with how you deal with a variety of social and economic problems in the world around you. Often, if your reference group is very small, then only within that group is it us, and the rest of the universe is them. At first I was concerned with getting free, but when I realized that my freedom was not independent of everybody else's, I understood that we can work on ourselves as a gift to other people so that we don't create more suffering for others.

You and I are the force for the transformation in the world. We are the consciousness that will define the nature of the reality we are moving into. Shifting our consciousness has the power to change our inner and outer universe. That's why you work on yourself. That's what help you offer. You work on yourself through everything in your life. Conscious social action includes our own work on ourselves that becomes the vehicle for our awakening.

SATSANG

Satsang or *sangha* is a crucial aspect of our *sadhana*, our spiritual practice. Satsang is a community of truth seekers. It's a group of people with the shared awareness that there's a spiritual dimension to the universe. Satsang is a group of people seeking truth who get together and share food, share kirtan and chant together, share stories, study spiritual texts, meditate together, and provide spiritual support for one another. I treasure it. It's family. Satsang is beautiful. SATSANG BECOMES OUR SOUL POD, WHERE WE CAN DEEPEN IN COMMUNITY WITH OTHER SOULS WHO ARE ALSO EXPLORING A SIMILAR PATH. It's not something you often feel within your biological family. It's a family of the heart that we share many lifetimes with. We all have different guises and costumes, and appear on stage in different scenes, playing different characters. We're all parts of the jigsaw puzzle of each other's karma. I think we are all on a journey, and what we can do is we can give each other confidence, we can help each other along.

I used to feel badly for people that had no satsang. I used to tell people to go all around their surrounding area to find satsang. Now the Internet is also satsang. The Internet provides worldwide satsangs. It's expanding our connections and helping people find a spiritual community where they feel respected, nurtured, and inspired to appreciate each other, to learn and grow as spiritual beings.

It takes courage to be truthful about yourself, who you are and what's going on, and to use that truth for personal growth. That's risk-taking. It's a big risk to identify with your soul, to see others as souls, to see yourself as and to be loving awareness. It's OK to do that in satsang, but always trust your intuition if something doesn't feel right. Your satsang can be a support system that allows you to take this risk to talk to people honestly and truthfully, and to take a risk to open your heart. Maharajji said, "Courage is a really important thing." And so is satsang.

When you go out into the woods, and you look at trees, you see all these different trees. And some of them are bent, and some of them are straight, and some of them are evergreens, and some of them are whatever. And you look at the tree and you allow it. You see why it is the way it is. You sort of understand that it didn't get enough light, and so it turned that way. And you don't get all emotional about it. You just allow it. You appreciate the tree.

The minute you get near humans, you lose all that. And you are constantly saying, "You are too this," or, "I'm too this." That judgment mind comes in. And so I practice turning people into trees. Which means appreciating them just the way they are.

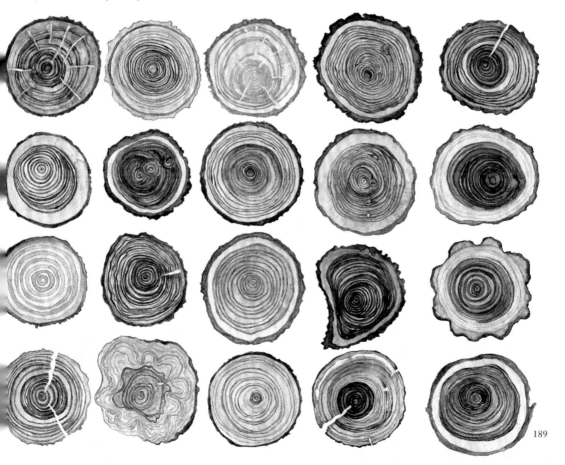

FEED EVERYONE
GOD COMES TO THE HUNGRY IN THE FORM OF FOOD.

Maharajji said that feeding the hungry and remembering God was the path to enlightenment. He said, "Feed everyone as a way to awaken. Food is God. Feeding the hungry is actually worship." He said hunger distracts the mind from focusing on spiritual thoughts.

You feed your body so that you can maintain it as a temple, so that you can deepen your wisdom, so that you can increase your concentration, so that you can get through your ego, so that you can come to a higher consciousness. Far out! And that *includes* having that pizza. I mean, it's *all* of it. Everything you eat becomes your offering of service. That becomes what eating is all about for you. Just notice your action, without judgment; notice what it is you're offering to God.

In many temples and ashrams, you never cook food without a mantra. You always have something you're saying inside to remind you that you're not just cooking food, you are doing a part of the divine process that is keeping the body and the temple maintained and nurturing life. That's what the journey is. The *Bahagavad Gita*, Hindu scripture from the first millennium BCE, says, "Do what you do, but dedicate the fruits of your work for me." Cooking food can be a spiritual endeavor, and a way to connect to a higher consciousness.

COOKING WITH YOUR OWN HANDS AND FEEDING PEOPLE IS THE HIGHEST FORM OF SADHANA, OR SPIRITUAL PRACTICE. Maharajji said, "It is not easy to cook food. You have to give your full attention to it, and only then will it turn out well."

Before eating, I would bless my food. For many people, saying grace in childhood was a time of impatience when adults were controlling the situation, but I discovered that it can become a moment to reawaken a living truth. I would hold the food up or sit with my hands beside my plate and say a blessing. Then I would just think about it for a moment and realize that this whole ritual of praying over food is part of the universe. The food I was praying over, the bowl of oatmeal or whatever I was

ASHRAM CHAI RECIPE

From the kitchen of the Neem Karoli Baba Ashram, Taos, New Mexico

4 cups water
4 cups milk (or dairy substitute)
3 teaspoon cardamom pods, crushed
$\frac{1}{2}$ cup crushed fresh ginger
$\frac{1}{4}$ cup loose leaf black tea
$\frac{1}{4}$ cup sugar

Add crushed ginger to water, bring to a boil for 15 minutes, cover pot. Add crushed cardamom pods and boil for an additional 5 minutes. Remove from heat, add black tea, cover and steep for 10 minutes. In a separate pot, heat milk and sugar until it froths, then remove from heat. Strain tea and spice mixture into hot milk. Jai guru dev!

eating, is part of God. The natural elements required for the food to grow and the farmers who grew and harvested the food were also part of God. I, who was making this prayer and offering up this food, am also part of God. And the hunger that I was using the oatmeal to quiet, the pangs in my stomach, the desires, the fire that will consume this food, that's also part of God. And I began to sense the oneness of everything. I came to understand that the deeper I appreciate that it's All One, the deeper I become one with All, and sense that all separateness is over.

I would say a blessing over my food all the time to remind me of this, to bring me home. I got to a point where I really couldn't sit down to a meal without doing this. Sometimes in a restaurant I would just sit quietly and go inward. I didn't have to make a production out of it. I didn't have to stop other people from eating.

So I suggest that the next time you are waiting for food to be served, feeling impatient or hungry, that you use it as a chance to think of the source of creation. And then when you receive the food, say a blessing and let the food remind you that All is One. Then eat.

Rituals can become rigid things, or they can become loose things. Slowly over time this ritual becomes a living statement of our connection to the divine, of our unity with everything manifest in the universe.

NEEM KAROLI BABA

Maharajji was often called Baba, a Hindi term meaning father or grandfather but used as an honorific; for example, Neem Karoli Baba. He is a beloved Hindu guru and a devotee of Hanuman, the Hindu monkey god who embodies devotion and service. He was born around 1900 to a wealthy Brahmin family in the village of Akbarpur in Uttar Pradesh, India, and was given the name Lakshman Narayan Sharma. When he was eleven years old, and just married, he left home to become a wandering sadhu, or holy person. Later in life, at his father's urging, he came back home to focus on married life. He had two sons and a daughter, but continued to practice bhakti yoga, known as the path of the heart, or loving devotion to God, and inspired others to live a life of seva, of service, as the highest form of devotion to God.

Maharajji, wrapped in his plaid blanket, often said "Sub Ek," meaning All is One. HE TAUGHT SIMPLY TO LOVE EVERYONE, SERVE EVERYONE, REMEMBER GOD, AND TELL THE TRUTH. Neem Karoli Baba said that attachments and ego in the physical body are the greatest obstacles to becoming free from suffering. He spent all his life helping and serving people, feeding them, and just loving all of humanity unconditionally. He was known as "Miracle Baba" throughout northern India and throughout the world because of his powers like mind reading, being in two places at once, and performing other miracles. He is pure light, pure love, pure energy. He left his body on the eleventh of September in 1973.

Maharajji's miracles continue to this day. When devotees remember him, he appears. Even though he died decades ago, it is said that he continues to visit, help, protect, guide, feed, and inspire people to live a life of love and service. He is honored and remembered by millions across the globe with the same unconditional love he offered to all.

Some of Maharajji's ashrams are in Kainchi, Vrindavan, Rishikesh, Shimla, Neem Karoli village near Khimasepur in Farrukhabad, Bhumia Dhar, Hanuman Garhi, and Delhi in India; and in America in Taos, New Mexico.

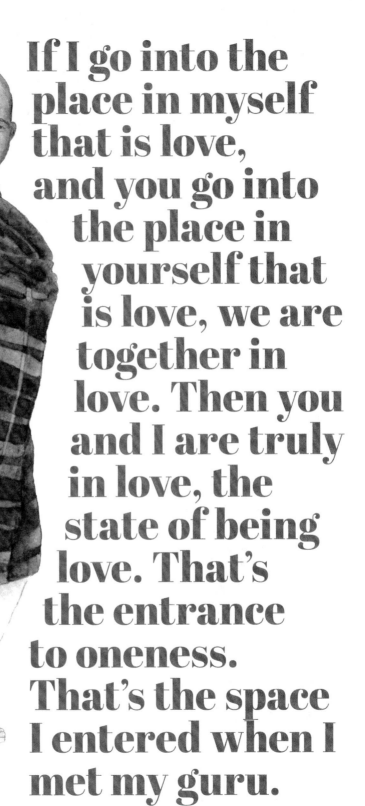

If I go into the place in myself that is love, and you go into the place in yourself that is love, we are together in love. Then you and I are truly in love, the state of being love. That's the entrance to oneness. That's the space I entered when I met my guru.

SRI SIDDHI MA

Sri Siddhi Ma, also referred to as Ma or Mataji, meaning respected mother, was a very close devotee of Maharajji and is seen as a great saint and yogini. After her husband died and her children had all grown up, she lived full-time at Maharajji's ashrams, along with other Mas, including Sri Jivanti Ma and some of the other women devotees. However, she remained mostly out of sight until Neem Karoli Baba's passing. After Maharajji left his body in 1973, Sri Siddhi Ma blessed all of his ashrams with a quiet and compassionate leadership. She carried on Maharajji's legacy of nurturing souls and made sure that his ashrams and temples were lovingly cared for as sacred containers.

For an hour every morning, Maharajji would fill a few pages in his diary with the name of God. Days before his death, he gave his diary to Siddhi Ma and told her, "Now this is your book. You write in it." She continued this daily practice and Maharajji's work with love and devotion.

Since the time that Maharajji left his body, he started manifesting more and more through Siddhi Ma's transmission. SHE CONVEYED THE LOVE THAT MAHARAJJI IS; SHE WAS AN EXTENSION OF HIS UNCONDITIONAL LOVE. We in the satsang will throw off our attachments and meet her in her true self, the Soul. For those who felt protected by her, that protection will continue. We all remain under her umbrella of grace. It was clear to me that when Maharajji left his body he was ever present. And in this same way, I feel joyful for this transition of Siddhi Ma. Although her name means Mother of Spiritual Power, for all of us, her spiritual family, she is simply Ma. She left her body on December 28, 2017. Her blessings, both hidden and revealed, are received with gratitude by all who honor and love her.

There have been consecrations of two temples for Sri Siddhi Ma, one at Kainchi Dham in Nainital, India and the second in Rishikesh, India, and a sacred shrine in Taos, New Mexico.

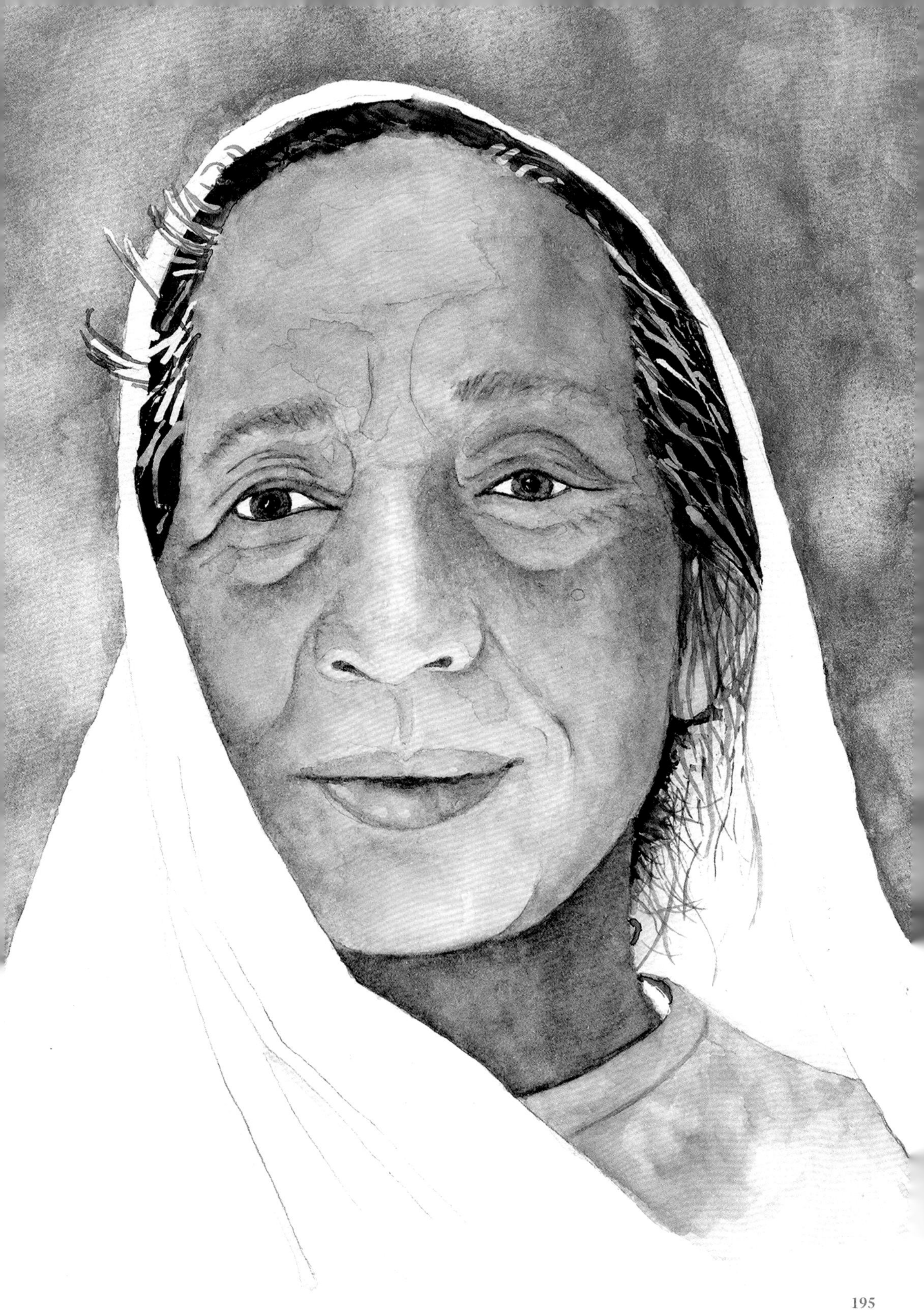

BIBLIOGRAPHY

Books

- *The Psychedelic Experience: A Manual Based on the Tibetan Book of the Dead* (with Timothy Leary and Ralph Metzner) (1964)
- *LSD* (with Sidney Cohen) (1966)
- *Be Here Now* (1971)
- *Doing Your Own Being* (1973)
- *The Only Dance There Is* (1974)
- *Grist for the Mill* (with Stephen Levine) (1977)
- *Journey of Awakening: A Meditator's Guidebook* (1978)
- *Miracle of Love: Stories About Neem Karoli Baba* (1978)
- *How Can I Help? Stories and Reflections on Service* (with Paul Gorman) (1985)
- *Compassion in Action: Setting Out on the Path of Service* (with Mirabai Bush) (1992)
- *Still Here: Embracing Aging, Changing and Dying* (2000)
- *One-Liners: A Mini-Manual for a Spiritual Life* (2002)
- *Paths to God: Living the Bhagavad Gita* (2004)
- *Be Love Now* (with Rameshwar Das) (2010)
- *Polishing the Mirror: How to Live from Your Spiritual Heart* (with Rameshwar Das) (2013)
- *Cookbook for Awakening: Core Teachings From Ram Dass* (2017)
- *Changing Lenses: Essential Teaching Stories from Ram Dass* (2018)
- *Walking Each Other Home: Conversations on Loving and Dying* (with Mirabai Bush) (2018)
- *Being Ram Dass* (with Rameshwar Das) (2021)
- *Reflections on the Journey: A Ram Dass Inspired Journal* (2021)
- *Words of Wisdom: Quotations From One of the World's Foremost Spiritual Teachers* (2021)

Films
- *A Change of Heart* (1994). PBS documentary, social action as a meditative act. Directed by Eric Taylor and hosted by Ram Dass.
- *Ecstatic States* (1996). Interview. Produced by Wiseone Edutainment Pty.
- *Ram Dass, Fierce Grace* (2001). Biographical documentary. Directed by Mickey Lemle.
- *Ram Dass – Love Serve Remember* (2010). Short film included in the *Be Here Now Enhanced Edition* e-Book. Directed by V. Owen Bush.
- *Dying to Know: Ram Dass & Timothy Leary* (2014). Documentary, portrait of Ram Dass and Timothy Leary and their friendship.
- *Ram Dass, Going Home* (2017). documentary portrait of Ram Dass in his later years, Directed by Derek Peck.
- *Ram Dass, Becoming Nobody* (2019). Documentary portrait of Richard Alpert becoming Ram Dass and Ram Dass becoming nobody. Directed by Jamie Catto.

Websites
- www.ramdass.org
- www.beherenownetwork.com
- www.nkbashram.org
- www.hanumanmaui.org
- www.lamafoundation.org
- www.seva.org

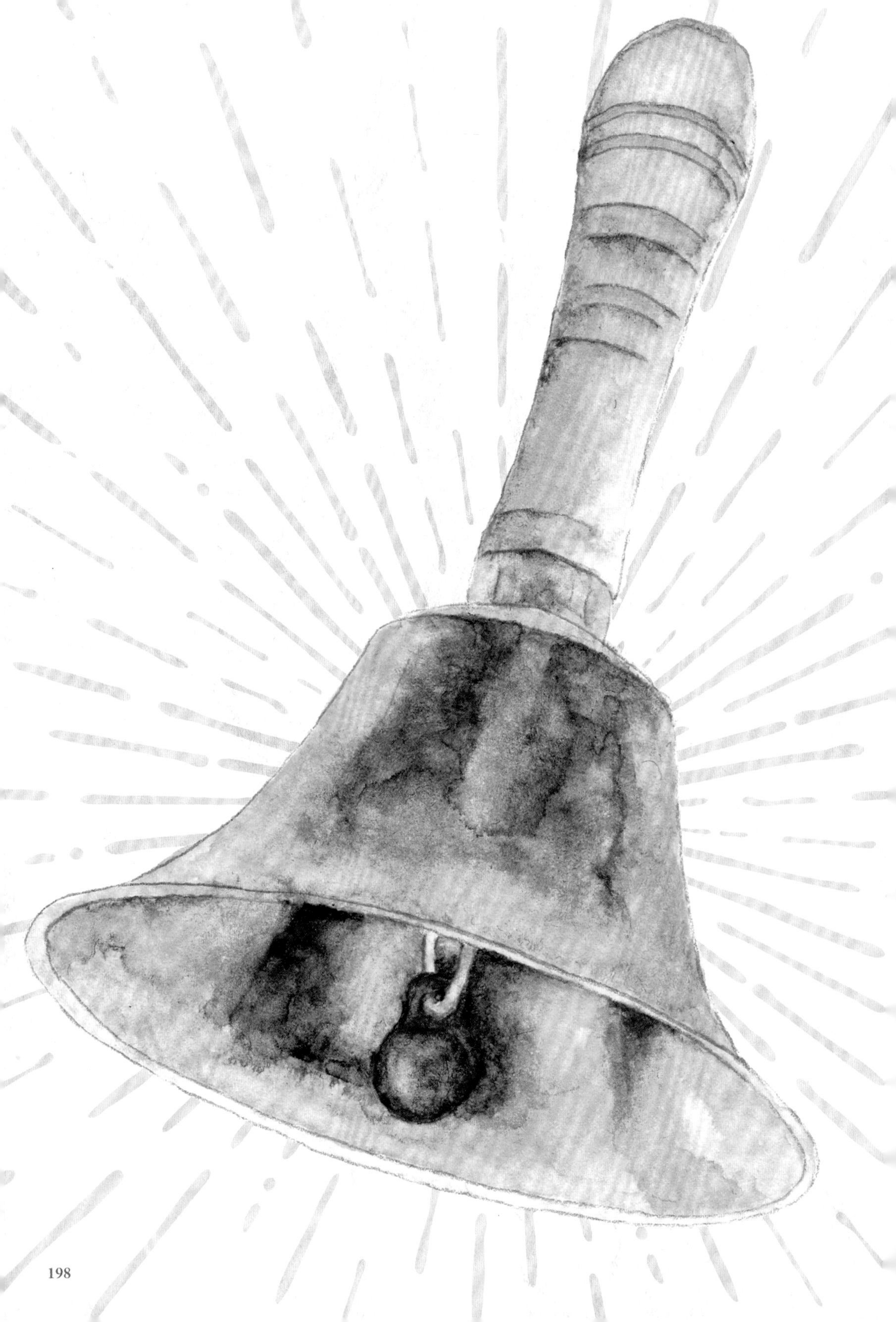

I wish you,
I wish for you,
grace.
Grace in your
lives.
-Ram Dass

September 27, 2019

Dear Baba Ram Dass,

We have our separate journeys of discovering your teachings in the 1990s, and first coming to the Neem Karoli Baba Ashram in Taos a few years later. As teenagers, we began exploring the mystical elements of our faith and getting to know our true selves. We learned from your personal story and searched deeper behind your words. Your perspective arrived at the perfect time in our lives. It was no accident that we both ended up living a short drive from the ashram.

Be Here Now, How Can I Help, Paths to God, Polishing the Mirror, and many of your books, recordings and group retreats have been invaluable for us and millions of others. Over the years we've been blessed to sit at your feet in Maui and Taos. With endless gratitude, we have applied your wisdom to all aspects of our lives.

We hope we've highlighted your teachings in such a way that this book will be a meaningful resource for spiritual explorers of all ages, everywhere.

In loving awareness,

Amy & Julie

Photo Credit: Kathleen Dassima Murphy

WITH A HEART FULL OF GRATITUDE, WE OFFER OUR THANKS TO THE FOLLOWING:

Ram Dass, Neem Karoli Baba and Sri Siddhi Ma for their wisdom, grace and unconditional love.

Julian, Josh, Izaak, Mars, Deva, Reuben and Courtney for their love, support, contributions and technical expertise.

Mirabai Starr for her hand in this project and nurturing friendship.

The Love Serve Remember Foundation, Rameshwar Das, and especially Raghu Markus and Rachael Fisher for their blessing and partnership.

Jenny Silbert for her creative inspiration, guidance and love.

Castille Aguilar, Bodhi Bird-Maqubela, Jacquelyn Dobrinska, Evan Geisler, Mindy McGovern, Sunshine Muse, Nicole Schiller, Scott Seine, and Jesse Wood for their helpful feedback; Wendy Young for her incredible assistance; Alan Dino Hebel and Ian Koviak at theBookDesigners; Katie Killebrew and Amanda Nelson, and friends at Mandala Publishing, Insight Editions and Simon & Schuster; and *you*, dear reader.

RAM DASS, formerly Dr. Richard Alpert, became a multigenerational spiritual teacher and cultural icon from the 1960s through 2019, when he passed away at his home on Maui. His revolutionary book *Be Here Now* made Eastern spiritual traditions and practices more accessible to a Western audience. After a near-fatal stroke, Ram Dass spent the remainder of his life on Maui, continuing to write books, share teachings, and hold retreats. Ram Dass devoted his life to service, founding the Love Serve Remember Foundation, the Hanuman Foundation, and cofounding the Seva Foundation, and the Neem Karoli Baba Ashram in Taos, New Mexico.

AMY BUETENS is an artist, illustrator and art educator. She is a certified integrative thanatologist and death educator. Her work includes performing final rites of passage, and she serves as a leader in her Jewish burial society. She has been a dedicated student of Ram Dass for over 20 years, and is a co-leader for the Love Serve Remember Foundation's International Women's Satang and leads her local Ram Dass Fellowship.

JULIE WEINSTEIN'S professional career is devoted to advancing environmental and social justice. She also serves as both a Jewish and Buddhist chaplain in the jails, within the justice movement and for people experiencing loss, grief and trauma. She is a death educator, burial society leader, and artist, and is pursuing ordination as a Rabbinic Pastor. She's been practicing Ram Dass's teachings for over two decades, and co-leads community initiatives for the Love Serve Remember Foundation.

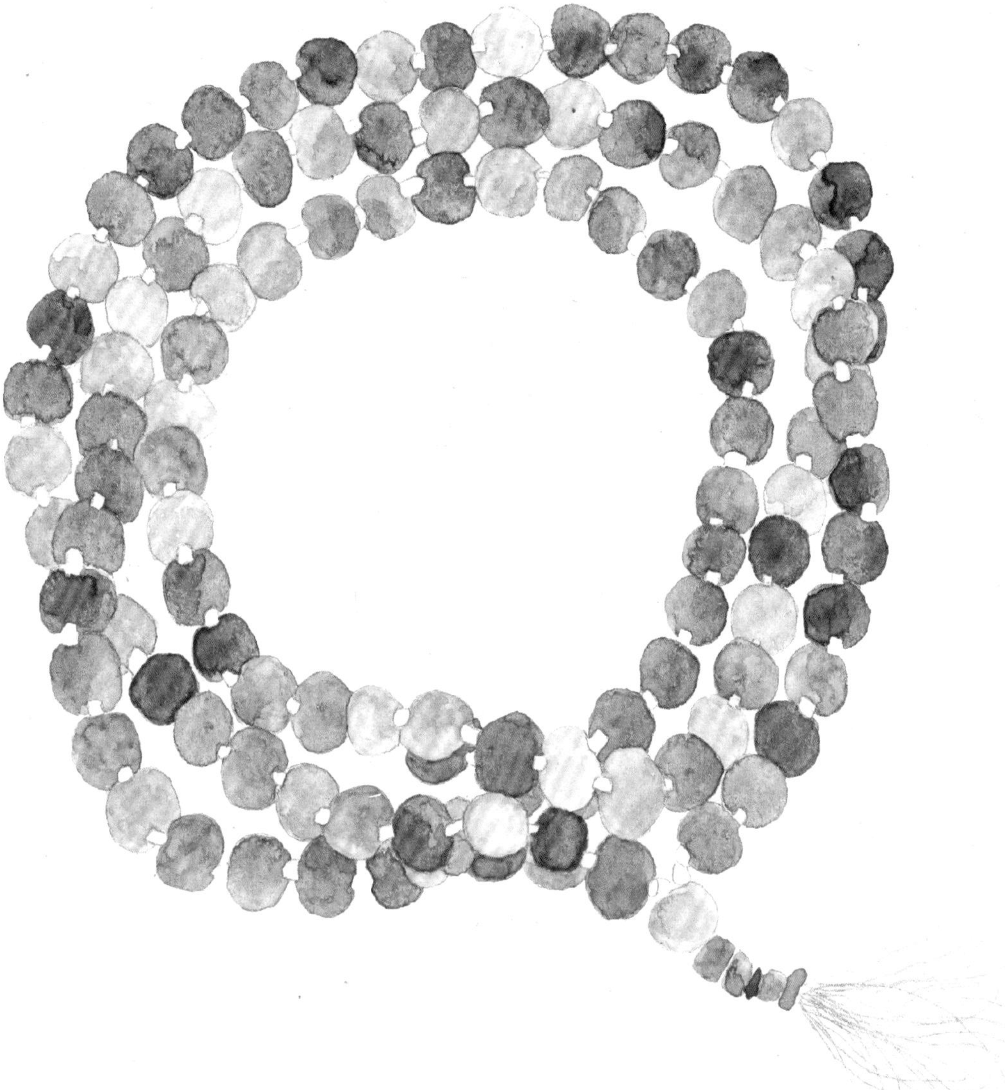